Autism:
A Holistic View

Regina Varin-Mignano, LCSW-R

Copyright ©2008 Regina Varin-Mignano – All rights reserved.

No part of this publication either text or image may be used for any purpose other than personal use, except as permitted under Section 107 or 108 under the 1976 United States Copyright act. Therefore, reproduction, modification, storage in a retrieval system or retransmission, in any form or by any means, electronic, mechanical or otherwise, for reasons other than personal use, is strictly prohibited without prior written permission.

For Christopher, Michael and Paul

Special thanks to Yolanda Vitulli and the staff at Tender Care Human Services, Inc, Adelphi University School of Social Work, the Social Work Department at Queens Hospital Center and all the families and consumers with whom I have interacted over the years. You were my inspiration to write this book.

TABLE OF CONTENTS

Introduction
　　………………………………………………….Page 7

Chapter 1: Past and Present History
　　………………………………………………….Page 17

Chapter 2: Autism and the Holistic View in Social Work
　　………………………………………………….Page 27

Chapter 3: Biological Aspects
　　………………………………………………….Page 42

Chapter 4: Past and Present Policies
　　………………………………………………… Page 59

Chapter 5: Social Aspects of Autism
　　………………………………………………….Page 75

Chapter 6: Autism and the Family
　　………………………………………………….Page 93

Chapter 7: Summary and Recommendations
　　………………………………………………….Page 109

Chapter 8: Autism Resources
　　………………………………………………….Page 125

Bibliography
　　………………………………………………….Page 152

INTRODUCTION

"If every person took a few moments to look back over their life they might come to recall one special time when they realized that there was a meaning to life that they had never considered. That moment for me is when I am able to help a patient/family learn about what is available to them, and facilitate for them the resources that can maintain their independence and dignity as a human being. Each one of these moments gives me my greatest accomplishment - gaining a deeper understanding of life so as to bring comfort to myself and others who are under stress." - R.V.M.

Much of the recent research in autism comes from a quantitative, researcher's viewpoint. However, this book's mission is to look at the "whole picture" in order to capture the meaning of Autism and its effects on the family. The book is written primarily for social work professionals in the field of autism and developmental disabilities, Students, individuals affected with Autism Spectrum Disorders and their families alike, and anyone who has a special interest in the ASD field.

In order to capture the impact of autism, one needs to look at all the different aspects that make up the culture of autism: its history, the biological and environmental aspects; past and present governmental and educational policies; the social impact of autism and its impact on the family unit. In attempting to understand a problem in social functioning, a social worker, like myself, cannot achieve understanding by adding together the assessment of the individual and the environment, but must strive for a full understanding of the complex interactions between the autistic individual and his/her environment. Holism in social work also has given further rise to family systems theory of treatment – by looking at a family unit as an open system or as a closed system by the amount of therapeutic intervention they receive and the level of growth that they achieve. In the development and writing of this book, I stayed consistent with the holistic theory by utilizing my own personal experiences as a mother with a now 21 year old son with Tourette's Syndrome and Asperger's Disorder, and my professional experiences as a social worker and now educator in the field. I feel that this personal experience enhances what I have learned through education and work experience, and provides a different perception on how to manage and succeed with your child.

My Story:

Throughout my formative years I was the quiet and smart kid who never caused any trouble and did her school work. I was also teased, because I was considered somewhat awkward and nerdy (I was an avid mathematician and chess player) and not part of many of the Long Island "girl clicks" that was around those days. I was somewhat isolated and alone, and ironically preferred it that way – I felt freer to do and explore what I wanted to do. I started to break out of my shell when I was about 16 years old, around the time I met my son's father. As any typical teenage girl would do, I wore a little makeup and started dressing more fashionably, listened to popular music, and cut my hair (which I insisted on growing until it was nearly three feet long). Here I was a High School Honor Student with my first boyfriend and finally feeling like I was part of something. I felt almost invincible – until I got pregnant. My whole world came crashing down around me. My boyfriend (and son's father) left the state with the help of his mother and never acknowledged his child nor provided support. My parent's marriage was quickly deteriorating and my younger sisters were out of control. Luckily I had my Uncle, who helped me get back on my feet and encouraged me not to drop out of school, which I had no intention of doing in the first place. I graduated in the top 20 of my class with my son in arm, and then moved with my mother (who was now separated from my father) and younger sisters soon afterwards to live with my aunt and Uncle in Queens, N.Y. with my ailing grandmother to attend college. My mom helped me with my son so I can attend college and not loose the scholarship that I worked so hard for. I felt invincible again, but this time more responsible. I started out initially as a pre-med/microbiology major, but quickly changed to a psychology major so I could be home more with my son. I was also working part-time as a bookkeeper. I had attempted to obtain public assistance, but upon applying, I was treated so horribly and felt so degraded that I walked out and swore that I would try to stay off welfare as much as I could. During my undergraduate study at Long Island University, I acquired the necessary background knowledge by taking advanced courses in the areas of psychology and sociology, including sociological research methods, social theory, statistics, psychological research, and psychotherapy.

      My interest in autism actually began in 1988 with the film "The Rain Man" starring Dustin Hoffman and Tom Cruise. I remember how fascinated I was with Hoffman's Character and - ironically – nearly identified with him in some way. In my junior year I decided to do an independent research project on autism, not knowing that a year later my own son would receive that diagnosis. I remember how alone I felt when the CPSE team told me that my son, who was 3 1/2 years old, had "severe autism". Looking back, he did exhibit many of the typical behaviors: echolalia, preservative speech, poor eye contact, and lack of social skills but as a young mother I was not experienced enough to know the difference. I felt incredible despair, that I was being punished in some way. I was only 21 years old when I found out. I tried to explain it to my family and no one understood, they just thought that Michael (my son) was very smart. He was (and still is) very intelligent - Michael at the time was reading on a first grade level and his artistic skills were very advanced. However, I was in denial and, with the support of his pre-school teacher was able to have Michael re-evaluated and re-diagnosed with Pervasive Developmental Disorder, NOS. This evaluation helped Michael be able to be mainstreamed into a regular education classroom from kindergarten on, avoiding some of the struggles with the NYC special education system. Initially, I thought it would be helpful to inform teachers and other parents of Michael's diagnosis – so as to understand why Michael behaved the way he did (e.g.: poor eye contact, preservative behaviors). However, it had the reverse effect, they separated Michael from certain school activities (with and without my knowledge) and other children were told to avoid him. He was send home from school when he would "act up" to avoid being teased by the other children. I had complained but also lived in fear – fear that he would be placed into an inappropriate educational setting. It was his intelligence and strong academic skills, luckily, which prevented that from happening.

After Michael finished the fifth grade, I placed him American Martyr's Catholic School in Bayside, Queens. Prior to this Michael was also diagnosed with Tourette's Syndrome – which has a high co-morbidity rate with children with Asperger's disorder, of which he was also re-diagnosed with. I did inform the school of his Tourette's Syndrome, of which they were familiar with but knowingly kept the PDD/Asperger's Diagnosis from them. The teachers eventually found out (after Michael started kicking his shoes daily onto the school roof, because he "Had" too), but they accepted Michael no less than any other student in the school. It was the best decision that I ever made – Michael felt the "big heart" of this little school (there were less than 200 students in the school) and excelled both academically and socially. He went onto a catholic high school and graduated with honors. He was then awarded a Dominican Scholarship at Molloy College and is currently double majoring in Mathematics and Computer Science. His Tourette's tics have subsided somewhat, but the socialization issue is still present. However, he is coping well with it and is quite focused on going to graduate school. While going through all of this, I met and married my husband Chris and had another son (Paul) and went back to Adelphi University for my master's degree in social work (and my PhD in social work latter on as well). While perusing my graduate studies I acquired the necessary foundation skills in social work practice, social welfare and human behavior and by concentrating my studies in the areas of Social Policy within the health, chemical dependency and mental health services. In addition, my field internships at Queens Hospital Center's Psychiatric Day Treatment Program and Lifeline Center for Child Development School Program help me gain and utilize intake, evaluation, assessment, and termination skills in working with clients and their families. These internships also helped me in learning how to participate in multidisciplinary team conferences and parent staff conferences and network with other professionals and departments within the organizational system of the agency.

    I strengthened and further developed my leadership and professional "autism" experience at QSAC – Quality-of-Life and services for the Autism Community. I started out as a service coordinator and eventually became the assistant director of Case Management, where I supervised 12 Case Managers, each with maximum Caseload of 25 Autistic consumers and their families. I learned that, due to the nature of the autistic consumer, most contact is with the consumer's family – which could become difficult at times. A case manager/social worker would need to have the ability to "Tune-In" to the individual and family's needs prior to a scheduled visit and have strong assessment skills to develop a service plan. I also presided in the administration and Provision of the Case Management, Respite, Family Reimbursement, Respite, and After School Programs. These programs were designed to provide support, respite, and "relief" to the parent or caregiver of the autistic child or adult. Teaching came hand in hand in my supervision of the case management staff, educating the staff on client services, and special and unique needs as well as development of treatment plans, utilizing therapeutic skills in the areas of contracting, confronting and reframing with families, and maximizing the independence, integration, and individualization of the Autistic Consumer. This proved to be an invaluable experience, which helped and led me to assist in the formation and Serve on the Board of a Non-Profit organization that serves the Autistic and Developmentally Disabled in the Queens Borough – Tender Care Human Services, Incorporated. Here, I have assisted in the implementation of programs and services, grant writing, fund raising, and working on a macro level with other social service and governmental agencies. I am still an active member of the advisory board to this day

This knowledge base helped me in my next position as a Medical Social Worker at Queens Hospital Center, where I stayed for over nine years. Here, I conducted psychosocial assessments, formulated discharge planning and counseling to patients and families from a wide variety of ethnic, religious and economic backgrounds. Queens Hospital, being a city hospital, receives many of the "unwanted" patients that many private hospitals quietly shun away from (alcoholics, mentally ill, mentally disabled, uninsured, and elderly.) Many victims of domestic violence, sexual assault, child and elder abuse/neglect, enter through the emergency room and impatient floors of Queens Hospital Center as well, therefore giving me a "broad" base of experience with the many social issues of society. Frequently, many of these patients are individuals over 65 years of age or disabled with multiple medical and social issues. Many social policies that are currently in place for the elderly and the disabled are somewhat helpful but not supportive enough for this population, therefore sometimes makes the process of assisting families difficult. For example, many autistic and developmentally disabled adults, who resided with aging parents, were commonly brought to the emergency room and admitted as a "social disposition" case. This was due to either poor long term care planning for placement on the parent's part, or the parent finally admitting that they can no longer manage the behaviors of their adult child. For parents who planned in advance for placement with their adult child, many were faced with the red-tape of group home placement (New York State is quite difficult to find residential placement) and had become frustrated with the system. This experience helped me in further understanding of the family of the autistic child, and my further desire to pursue my PhD in social work, studying the mothers of autistic children and their coping responses relative to the support they receive. As of August, 2007, I became the coordinator of the Office of Student with disabilities at CUNY-York College, where we assist disabled students with accommodations to meet their educational needs. Some of these students are students with Asperger's disorder, which has presented a new venue of study in the autism field.

In order to address some of the issues from my professional experience, this book has been broken down into the following chapters: Chapter 1: The past and present history on autism. This gives a historical overview on autism as a spectrum disorder. Chapter 2: Autism and social work, which expounds on the definition of holism and how it can be utilized in exploring the culture of autism and in the social work profession. Chapter 3: Biological aspects of autism, which focuses on different causes and treatments for the autistic disorder. Chapter 4: Past and present governmental and educational policies regarding autism. Chapter 5: The social aspects of autism. This chapter speaks about the social aspects and resources that are available (or could be available for the autistic consumer and their family. Chapter 6: Stress and the family – which looks at the effects of caring for the autistic child on the family unit and Chapter 7: Summary and recommendations that I feel would be helpful in helping an individual with autism spectrum disorder and their family. Lastly, Chapter 8 is dedicated to provide the reader with some useful resources in regards to autism. It is not a comprehensive list, but enough just to get some one familiar with the resources that are available.

CHAPTER 1:

AUTISM SPECTRUM DISORDERS: PAST AND CURRENT KNOWLEDGE

Not until the middle of the twentieth century was there a name for a disorder that now appears to affect an estimated 1 out of every 166 children ages 3-10, a disorder that causes disruption in families and unfulfilled lives for many children. Autistic disorder, the best known of the disorders, is characterized by sustained impairment in reciprocal social interactions, communications and stereotypical behavioral patterns. (Kaplan, 1994) Infantile autism was a term coined by Leo Kanner in 1943 but it was not until 1980, in the third edition of the DSM that autistic disorder was recognized as a distinct clinical entity. Kanner suspected the syndrome to be more frequent than it seemed and suggested that some children had been misclassified as mentally retarded or with childhood schizophrenia. (Kaplan, 1994) However, in Kanner's research, he described that these children had exceptional, almost savant-like, rote memory and normal physical appearance. Kanner concluded that these children were capable of achieving normal cognitive abilities. At the same time a German scientist, Dr. Hans Asperger, described a milder form of the disorder that became known as Asperger syndrome. Thus these two disorders were described and are today listed in the *Diagnostic and Statistical Manual of Mental Disorders* DSM-IV-TR (fourth edition, text revision) as two of the five pervasive developmental disorders (PDD), more often referred to today as autism spectrum disorders (ASD). The Pervasive Developmental

Disorders (or PDD) are a group of psychiatric conditions in which expected social skills, language development, and normal childhood behaviors do not develop appropriately. In general, PDD affects multiple areas of development, are manifested early in life, and cause persistent dysfunction.

Historically, it was believed that parents of children with autism were overly intellectual, cold-hearted, and had a limited interest in other people. This psychoanalytic view of autism is based on the theory of Sigmund Freud, which was introduced in the 1930s and 1940s in the United States. According to this theory, autism is caused by a child's reaction to his family environment. In the 1960s Bruno Bettleheim, a child psychiatrist, wrote the "The Empty Fortress," a book about autism written from the psychoanalytic view that popularized the term "refrigerator mother." According to this theory, the cause of autism was believed to lie in a mother's unconscious rejection of her child. This theory was never supported by empirical research and has since been discredited by the professional autism research community. Until the Mid 1970's, treatment regiments involved helping parents, usually mothers, to become less rejective of their children. (Klinger/Dawson, 1996) However, that theory was dispelled when Dr. Bernard Rimland and Dr. Eric Schloper argued that the disorder was due to a neurological impairment. In practice, they disputed, psychodynamic theories place so much emphasis on the cold, unloving environment in which an autistic child has been raised causes stress for the parents without obtaining results for the child (Lovaas, 1979).

Autism Defined:

According to the fourth edition of the Diagnostic and Statistical Manual of Mental Disorders (DSM-IV-TR), Autism is now considered a developmental disability that typically appears during the first three years of life. The result of a neurological disorder that affects functioning of the brain, autism and its associated behaviors occur in approximately 2 to 5 cases per 10,000 individuals. Several autism-related disorders are also grouped under the broad heading "Pervasive Developmental Disorder" or PDD: PDD-NOS (pervasive developmental disorder, not otherwise specified), Asperger's syndrome and Rett's syndrome. These three diagnoses are used differently by professionals to describe individuals who manifest some, but not all, of the autism characteristics. The diagnosis of autism is made when a specified number of characteristics listed in the DSM-IV are present, in ranges inappropriate for the child's age. In contrast, a diagnosis of PDD-NOS may be made when a child exhibits fewer symptoms than in autism, although those symptoms may be exactly the same as a child with an autism diagnosis. Asperger's and Rett's syndrome display the most marked differences from autism. The following areas are among those that may be affected by autism:

1.) **Communication**: language develops slowly or not at all; uses of words without attaching the usual meaning to them; communicates with gestures instead of words; short attention spans

2.) **Social Interaction**: spends time alone rather than with others; shows little interest in making friends; less responsible to social cues such as eye contact or smiles

3.) **Sensory Impairment**: unusual reactions to physical sensations such as being overly sensitive to touch or under-responsive to pain; sight, hearing, touch, pain, smell, taste may be affected to a lesser or greater degree

4.) **Play**: lack of spontaneous or imaginative play; does not imitate others actions; doesn't initiate pretend games

5.) **Behaviors**: may be overactive or very passive; throw frequent tantrums for no apparent reason; may perseverate on a single item, idea or person; apparent lack of common sense; may show aggressive or violent behavior or injure self.

Contrary to popular understanding, many children and adults with autism make eye contact, show affection, smile and laugh, and show a variety of other emotions, but in varying degrees. Like other children, they respond to their environment in positive and negative ways. The autism may affect their range of responses and make it more difficult to control how their body and mind react. They live normal life spans and the behaviors associated with may change or disappear over time. Autism is four times more prevalent in boys than girls and knows no racial, ethnic or social boundaries. Early Studies suggested that a high Socio-Economic status was common in families with autistic children. However, later research shows that family income, lifestyle and educational levels do not affect the chance of autism's occurrence.

Autism is known to interfere with the normal development of the brain in the areas of reasoning, social interaction and communication skills. Children and adults with autism typically have deficiencies in verbal and non-verbal communication, social interactions and leisure or play activities. The disorder makes it hard for them to communicate with others and relate to the outside world. They may exhibit repeated body movements (hand flapping, rocking), unusual responses to people or attachments to objects and resist any changes in routines. In some cases, aggressive and/or self-injurious behavior may be present. In order to be diagnosed with autism, an individual must have eight of the following sixteen characteristics, all based on observation (as there are no medical tests per se by which to identify autism):

- Marked lack of awareness of the existence of feelings of others
- Absence of, or abnormal seeking of comfort at times of distress
- Absence of, or impaired imitation
- Impairment in making peer relationships
- Limited or No mode of communication such as communicative babbling, facial expression, gesture, mime or spoken language
- Abnormal non-verbal communication with eye to eye gaze, facial expressions or body posture
- Absent imaginative activity: play acting, adult roles, fantasy characters, lack of interest in imaginary events
- Abnormalities in speech production: volume, pitch, stress, rate, rhythm and intonation * Impairment in ability to initiate or sustain a conversation with others despite adequate speech
- Stereotyped body movements: hand flicking, twisting, spinning, head banging, complex whole body movements

- Persistent preoccupation with parts of objects
- Marked distress with changes in trivial aspects of environment such as a vase being moved from its usual spot
- Unreasonable insistence on following routines in precise detail
- Markedly restricted range of interests and a preoccupation with one narrow interest

Individuals with autism may have other disorders which affect the functioning of the brain, such as epilepsy, mental retardation, or genetic disorders, such as Fragile X Syndrome. In most cases, there is an associative diagnosis of mental retardation, commonly in the moderate to severe range. (DSM IV, p. 67) Approximately 25-30% may develop a seizure pattern at some period during life. Its prevalence rate now places it as the third most common developmental disability - more common than Down's syndrome. Yet the majority of the public, including many professionals in the medical, educational, and vocational fields are still unaware of how autism affects people and how to effectively work with individuals with autism.

Autism is often referred to as a spectrum disorder, meaning that the symptoms and characteristics of autism can present themselves in a wide variety of combinations, from mild to severe. Although autism is defined by a certain set of behaviors, children and adults can exhibit any combination of the behaviors in any degree of severity. Two children, both with a diagnosis of autism, can act very differently from one another. Medical researchers are exploring different explanations for the various forms of autism. Although one specific cause of autism is not known, current research links autism to biological or neurological differences in the brain. MRI (Magnetic Resonance Imaging) and PET (Positron Emission Topography) scans show abnormalities in the structure of the brain, with significant differences within the cerebellum, including the size and number of Purkinje cells. In some families there appears to be a pattern of autism or related disabilities, which suggests there may be a genetic basis to the disorder, although at this time no one gene has been directly linked to autism. A wide range of pre, peri, and post-natal conditions are thought to pre-dispose children to the development of autism, including maternal rubella, untreated fetal phenyuletunora, and tuberous sclerosis, anoxia during birth, encephalitis, infantile spasms and fragile X Syndrome. (Moroz, 1989)

There are no specific medical tests for diagnosing autism. A diagnosis is mainly based on observations of the child's communication, behavior and developmental levels. However, because many of the behaviors associated with autism are shared by other disorders, a doctor may complete various medical tests to rule out other possible causes.

Below are several diagnostic tools have been developed over the past few years to help professionals make an accurate autism diagnosis:

CHAT - Checklist for Autism in Toddlers

CARS - Childhood Autism Rating Scale

PIA - Parent Interviews for Autism

GARS - Gilliam Autism Rating Scale

BRIAC - Behavior Rating Instrument for Autistic and other Atypical Children (Kaplan, 1994).

A brief observation in a single setting cannot present a true picture of an individual's abilities and behaviors. At first glance, the person with autism may appear to have mental retardation, a behavior disorder, or even problems with hearing. However, it is important also to distinguish autism from other conditions, since an accurate diagnosis can provide the basis for building an appropriate and effective educational and treatment program.

There are great differences among people with autism. Some individuals mildly affected may exhibit only slight delays in language and greater challenges with social interactions. They may have average or above average verbal, memory or spatial skills but find it difficult to be imaginative or join in a game of softball with their friends. Others more severely affected may need greater assistance in handling day to day activities like crossing the street or making a purchase.

Autism is four times more prevalent in boys than girls and knows no racial, ethnic or social boundaries. Early studies suggested that a high socio-economic status was common in families with autistic children. However, later research shows that family income, lifestyle and educational levels do not affect the chance of autism's occurrence. According to the U.S Census Bureau – U.S Department of Education Office of Special Education Programs Data

Analysis Systems (2000) the number of children and youth with autism enrolled in schools increased from 19.1 thousand in 1994 to 65.4 thousand in 2000 nationwide, equivalent to 1.2% of the total special education population in the United States. (p. 159). This increase also reflects the increase in early intervention referral on a local and state level of children who are classified as "autistic" and require specialized services. However, the Autism Society of America feels that the country is in the midst of an Autism Epidemic. In California State, for example, it has been reported by the Centers foe Disease Control that the number of individuals diagnosed with severe autism and who are receiving services in that state jumped another 21 percent in 2002. According to the new data, an alarming 20,377 individuals with a diagnosis of autism were receiving services from the department as of the fourth quarter of 2002, compared with 16,802 individuals as of the fourth quarter of 2001. This study is also supported by Gottleb's (2003) study in Atlanta, Georgia found that 3.4 in every 1000 children aged 3 to 10 years had mild to severe autism, on the basis of a review of their medical records. Surveys before the mid-1980s had found that only 4 to 5 in every 10 000 children were affected. The researchers in the Atlanta study, from the federal Centers for Disease Control and Prevention, suggested that some of the increase was the result of widened definitions of the disorder, but the explanation for the rest of the increase was unknown. (p. 71).

CHAPTER 2:

AUTISM AND THE HOLISTIC VIEW IN SOCIAL WORK

Social work is concerned with helping individuals, families, groups and communities to enhance their individual and collective well-being. Social Work is the profession committed to the pursuit of social justice, to the enhancement of the quality of life, and to the development of the full potential of each individual, group and community in society. We do this by looking at things through holistic perspective, gathering all the pieces together to make a whole. The profession has much to offer parents and children coping with autism, given their traditional comprehensive focus on assisting individuals and families at bio-psycho-social levels. Research has shown that basing the aims and purpose of service delivery on the perspectives of family members coping with autism is vital to the sense of quality perceived by the family (Heller, Miller, &Hsieh, 1999). Understanding the perceptions held by parents is vitally important to social work practitioners and researchers for the advancement of practice with autistic children.

In order to better understand how the holistic view would be helpful for children and adults diagnosed with autism and their families, I thought it would be helpful to give an explanation on Holism – which is what social worker, like myself, utilize in our practice and how it can be helpful in understanding autism and navigating the sea of information that is out there

What is Holism?

Holism, as defined in Random House –Webster's New Dictionary (1998) is the whole entities are more than the sum of their parts. Holism is a theory of knowledge that gives its attention to the organization or structure of a system and to the modes of information exchange that occurs within a system and with its environment. The overall essence of holism is that wholes have properties that cannot be explained in terms of their constituent parts or the relations between those parts. In looking at it from an organic point of view, a plant or animal is taken as a type of whole, with the fundamental holistic characters as a unity of parts, which is so close and intense as to be more than a sum of its parts.

Holism as an idea or philosophical concept is diametrically opposed to atomism. Where the atomist believes that any whole can be broken down or analyzed into its separate parts and the relationships between them, the holist maintains that the whole is primary and often greater than the sum of its parts. The atomist divides things up in order to know them better; the holist looks at things or systems in aggregate and argues that we can know more about them viewed as such, and better understand their nature and their purpose. In this context holism is to be understood as the view that human social groupings are greater than the sum of their members, that such groupings are 'organic' entities in their own right, that they act on their human members and shape their destinies, and that they are subject to their own independent laws of development (1976, p.33). Historicism, a paradigm shift from holism, is the belief that history develops inexorably and necessarily according to certain principles or rules towards a determinate end. The link between holism and historicism is that the holist believes that individuals are essentially formed by the social groupings to which they belong; while the historicist - who is usually also a holist - holds that we can understand such a social grouping only in terms of the internal principles, which determine its development. In Languages, holism plays a central and specific role in the understanding of them. Fodor and LePore (1992) distinguish three kinds of "meaning holism" in linguistics, which they call "content holism", "translation holism", and "anthropological holism". Content holism is the view that there can be no "small" systems: a mind or a language can contain one representation only if it contains many (p. 5). Content holism does not entail meaning holism, either, since it might be that any system must have many representations to qualify as a mind or language at all. Translation holism is the view that there can't be a positive but small amount of synonymy: two minds or languages can express one meaning in common only if they express many meanings in common (1992, p. 6). Meaning holism does not entail translation holism, since it is logically possible for two small systems to express all the same few meanings. Anthropological holism is the view that the meaning of a representation depends on nonrepresentational conditions, e.g., causal relations to represented things (1992, p. 6). Meaning holism without anthropological holism may claim that the meanings of "signs" are interdependent, but do not depend on anything besides signs.

As a general feature, holism is inherent in the humanism of social work. But in any specific field, the relations between the general, the specific and the particular are repeatedly institutionalized yet constantly shifting. It seems to be precisely in the tropes of turning toward the whole individual that the general and the special - the indefinite and the definite - can be substituted for each other. In this paper I will be discussing the concept of Holism as a theory of knowledge, what the theory seeks to achieve, its purpose and how it relates to social work knowledge of today. Although there have been many Holistic theorists postulating their concept of Holism, in this paper I will focus on three philosophers that had a major impact on the development of Holism as a knowledge base: Hegel, Durkheim, and Bertalanffy.

G.W.F. Hegel, the most influential and commonly thought of as the founder of Holism, belongs to the period of "German idealism" in the decades following Kant. The most systematic of the post-Kantian idealists, Hegel attempted, throughout his published writings as well as in his lectures, to elaborate a comprehensive and systematic ontology from a "logical" starting point. He is perhaps most well known for his teleological account of history, an account which was later taken over by Marx and culminating into communism. For most of the twentieth century, the "logical" side of Hegel's thought had been largely forgotten, but his political and social philosophy continued to find interest and support.

Hegel was born in Stuttgart in 1770, the son of an official in the government of the Duke of Württemberg. He was educated at the Royal High school in Stuttgart from 1777-88 and steeped in both the classics and the literature of the European Enlightenment. In October 1788 Hegel began studies at a theological seminary in Tübingen, the Tüberger Stift, where he became friends with the poet Hölderlin and philosopher Friedrich Schelling, both of whom would later become famous. In 1790 Hegel received an M.A. degree, one year after the fall of the Bastille in France. Shortly after graduation, Hegel became a tutor to a wealthy Swiss family in Berne from 1793-96. In 1797, Hegel moved to Frankfurt to take on another tutorship. During this time he wrote unpublished essays on religions, which display a certain radical tendency of thought in his critique of orthodox religion. In January 1801, two years after the death of his father, Hegel finished with tutoring and went to Jena where he took a position as a lecturer at the University of Jena, where Hegel's friend Schelling had already held a university professorship for three years. There Hegel collaborated with Schelling on a Critical Journal of Philosophy and he also published a piece on the differences between the philosophies of Fichte and Schelling in which preference was consistently expressed for the latter thinker. After having attained a professorship in 1805, Hegel published his first major work, the Phenomenology of Spirit (1807). With the closing of the University, Hegel had to seek employment elsewhere and so he took a job as editor of a newspaper in Bamberg, Bavaria in followed by a move to Nuremberg in 1808 where Hegel became headmaster of a preparatory school, and also taught philosophy to the students there until 1816. During this time Hegel married, had children, and published his Science of Logic in three volumes. One year following the defeat of Napoleon at Waterloo (1815), Hegel took the position of Professor of Philosophy at the University of Heidelberg where he published his first edition of the Encyclopedia of the Philosophical Sciences in Outline. In 1818 he became Professor of Philosophy at the University of Berlin, through the invitation of the Prussian minister von Altenstein and Hegel taught there until he died in 1831. Hegel lectured on various topics in philosophy, most notably on history, art, religion, and the history of philosophy and he became quite famous and influential. He held public positions as a member of the Royal Examination Commission of the Province of Brandenburg and also as a counselor in the Ministry of Education. In 1821 he published the Philosophy of Right and in 1830 was given the honor of being elected Rector of the University.

Hegel had mystical visions of the unity of all things, on which he based his own holistic philosophy of nature and the state. Nature consists of one timeless, unified, rational and spiritual reality. Hegel's state is a quasi-mystical collective, an "invisible and higher reality," from which participating individuals derive their authentic identity, and to which they owe their loyalty and obedience. However, it was Hegel's Philosophy of Mind (1817) and his Philosophy of History (1831) that strengthened the Logical principle and concept of Holism. Although there have been many examples in ancient

Greek and Roman Literature where the people and society are compared to a living person – an organic analogy, it was Hegel's common sense way of thinking that theorized the concept of Holism. As per Polkinghorne (1983) Hegel was concerned with a principle of "internal relations" through which he sought to correct our common sense conceptual framework. Hegel held that no particular constitutes a self sufficient independent unit, that any particular is what it is only because it stands in relationship to other units, each of which to some degree modifies its value, just as these are themselves modified in the process (p. 136). Hegel also believed that the concept of reasoning (which he called dialectical thinking or understanding) had the ability to move toward completeness, and considered a "whole entity" to be permeable and consistently growing and amending itself. In Hegel's view" both deductive and inductive logic are based on the notion of classifying, that is, they use concepts as definitions that bind together entities that possess the characteristics of concepts and exclude others" (p. 136). To explain simply, Hegel sees logic dealing with relations between classes and entities. How does this apply to a Holistic way of thinking? Well, an example I will use is our Doctoral class, which would be defined as an adding together of doctoral students to create a whole class, of which a "new characteristic" develops as a result of the relationship of the parts – my classmates – as we work together towards a common goal. Being part of a whole unit, respectively our class – requires "the use of dialectical thinking, which recognizes the new form of wholeness and that it consists of more than the sum of the parts which make it up" (p. 137).

A further example to illustrate Hegel's concept that the whole is more than its parts is the concept of emergent properties, or emergence. As per Phillips (1976) "the combination of atoms in the compound of water produces a substance of emergent properties. This is a case, organists argue, where the whole is clearly more than the sum of the parts- where the properties of the whole (the emergent water molecule) can only be discovered by studying the whole" (p. 14). By breaking down – in this case a water molecule – and then examining or analyzing these different parts, we would loose the qualities of what water is – or the characteristics of this "whole". Biologists also base Hegel's theory of knowledge on organic wholes and the theory of the evolution and development of these "wholes". There are forces within livening organisms, as Polkinghorne postulates, which could not be accounted for by examining the various parts. These forces drive organisms onward toward developing new forms. Biologists called their theory "creative evolution", which held that "evolution was the result of forces in the environment; creative evolution placed the cause of evolution within the organism itself" (p. 139).

Emile Durkheim (1858-1917) was another great philosopher who moved the Holistic perspective toward a Social or societal viewpoint. Durkheim was a French sociologist who was one of the pioneers in the development of modern sociology. He was born in Epinal in 1858, a decedent of a distinguished line of rabbinical scholars. He graduated from the Ecole Normale Superieure in Paris and then taught law and philosophy. In 1887, he began teaching sociology, first at the University of Bordeaux and later at the University of Paris. Durkheim believed that scientific methods should be applied to the study of society. He was also concerned with the basis of social stability – the common values shared by a society, such as morality and religion. In his view, these values, or the collective conscience, are the cohesive bonds that hold the social order together. A breakdown of these values, he believed, leads to a loss of social stability and to individual feelings of anxiety and dissatisfaction, sometimes resulting in suicide. As per Polkinghorne (1983) Durkheim's position is called Holism the opposite view is called "individualism" and it holds that all collective terms are analyzable and that hey refer to the complex pattern of behavior, beliefs, and attitudes of various people in certain situations (p. 141).

The question that Durkheim proposes is that does social group or societies have emergent properties as that of organisms? The use of Durkheim's application of Holistic Theory to social situations created a controversy between Holistic vs. individualistic methodology. Durkheim's viewed that individual persons have no part to play in the action of a social group. This is because he felt that their actions are determined by their own participation in the group. Durkheim, as stated by Polkinghorne (1983) points out one aspect of the Holistic approach to human phenomena – role theory.

Role Theory is defined as "a position occupied by a person in a group relative to other persons in that group. It carries with it certain expected regularities regarding the individual's behavior toward other members of the group and their behavior toward him or her; thus, the group entity controls the behavior of its parts by defining roles" (p. 142). In other words, individuals' behaviors are affected by the coercive power of the group, or the whole by performing a role in society.

Ludwig von Bertalanffy (1901--1972) was one of the most important theoretical biologists of the first half of this century; researched on comparative physiology, on biophysics, on cancer, on psychology, and on philosophy of science. He developed a kinetic theory of stationary open systems and the General System Theory, and was one of the founding fathers and vice-president of the Society for General System Theory, and one of the first who applied the holistic system methodology to psychology and the social sciences.

Ludwig von Bertalanffy was born in a little village near Vienna on September 19, 1901. In 1918 he started his studies with history of art and philosophy, firstly at the University of Innsbruck and then at the University of Vienna where he became a pupil of the philosophers Robert Reininger and Moritz Schlick, one of the founders of the Viennese Circle. He finished his PhD with a thesis on the German physicist and philosopher Gustav Theodor Fechner in 1926, and published his first book on theoretical biology, The Modern Theories of Development, two years later. In this he stated,

"Mechanism provides us with no group of the specific characteristics of organisms, of the organization of organic process among one another, of organic wholeness – of the problem of the origin of organic theology or of the historical characteristics of organisms" (p. 143). Bertalanffy created a paradigm shift from Hegel's and Durkheim's early theories of holism by expanding the notion of holism into a general theory about any whole and any system. Although Hegel attempted to develop a system for knowing the all, his answer to the question of holism has not found general acceptance. Von Bertalanffy maintained that systems were organized wholes and that they are not limited to organic or social entities, thus giving the framework for a general systems theory. According to Polkinghorne (1983) "the idea behind general systems theory is that there is a general ideal from which is isomorphic to all systems. This general form is called the object of inquiry, and the level of inquiry is the properties of systems, not specific systems themselves" (p. 143-144).

General Systems Theory is not limited to material systems but applies to any "Whole" consisting of individual parts and that it deals with living systems by identifying them as open systems with important inputs and outputs. As per Turner (1996) Von Bertalanffy goal "was to achieve a general perspective, a coherent view of the world as a great organization – a framework in which all disciplines could be understood in their place" (p. 604). Where Durkheim saw that individuals had defined roles that came under the cohesive power of the group, Bertalanffy's holistic systems view stresses the exchange of behaviors between people, and postulates circular causality – which emphasizes that forces do not simply move on one direction, but rather become part of a causal chain, each event influenced by the other. Initially, it was considered – as per theorists like Hegel – that the subsystems of a whole are isolated from the environment – in essence they were considered closed systems. Bertalanffy postulated an "open systems approach", which is central to general systems theory. "The open systems approach accounts for the continuing differentiation without contradicting the second law of thermodynamics. According to this approach, an open system receives substances from its environment and discharges into its environment" (p. 146). The open system does not depend on its initial state and that its final state will depend on the properties of the system, or whole itself – therefore allowing for growth within a whole. For example, the doctoral class would be considered an open system, because its members – my classmates – allow for increased knowledge and gives back knowledge (discharge) to the class as a whole, therefore allowing growth within the system.

How does Holism apply to the essential theory of knowledge in social work practice? As per Turner (1996) "social workers recognize the necessity of understanding the nature of the person-environment interrelatedness and the person situation transactions" (p. 605). Social workers are initially introduced to look at the client through a Bio-Psycho-Social perspective – focusing on the Biological, Social and Psychological functioning of a client. This is also emphasized in general systems theory as it relates to social work practice. There was a growing dissatisfaction with the mechanistic or analytical explanations in various branches of science, mathematics that had a significant impact on psychology development and social work theories. Kuhn (1996) proposed that the rapid growth of new knowledge in scientific disciplines is often triggered by new paradigms. Paradigm shifts such as Piaget's genetic epistemology, Carl Rodgers client centered therapy, Gestalt Psychology, as well as phenomenological and existential approaches recognized that systems, or "wholes" are capable of change and growth and rejected the individualists theory of independent study.

Bertalanffy's General Systems Theory assists the social worker by seeing the person "as a part of his or her total life relation; personal situations are a whole in which each part is interrelated to all other parts" (p. 605). In attempting to understand a problem in social functioning, a social worker cannot achieve understanding by adding together the assessment of the individual and the environment, but must strive for a full understanding of the complex interactions between the client and its environment. Holism in social work also has given further rise to family systems theory of treatment – by looking at a family unit as an open system or as a closed system by the amount of therapeutic intervention they receive and the level of growth that they achieve. Micro, Meso and Macro levels of practice in the social work field are also another example of holistic theory at work. As per Turner (1996) the macro level is common to most members of groups living in it and involves the physical, social, cultural and political structures of the larger society in which individuals grow up (p. 608). The meso level is the relationship of major groups that touch the daily life of the individual person, and the micro level focuses on the individual's own experience in social or "whole" situations. The Holistic paradigm contributes to understanding the dynamic web and interconnectedness of various relationships and offers hope that changes can occur at any level of any system by understanding the inter communication and interrelatedness of its parts. Furthermore, The Holistic approach, in social work and in other health care arenas, gives priority to relating to the whole person - body, mind, and spirit in a particular time, space and context. It is argued that the issue of a philosophical and moral base for holism is particularly crucial at a time when so-called market rationalism dominates not only in health care but also in an increasing range of human activities. "The discussion on a tension between the generally accepted theoretical move towards holism and the practical reality of applying holistic ideas in a society which continues to hold the scientific paradigm in high regard assumes that the difference between scientific and holistic is a principal one" (1998, p. 68). Both holistic educators and healers are now recognizing East and West differences in philosophies, healing schools and educational traditions, as well as their merging properties. In the Western countries, spirituality and humanistic psychology have been widely used as treatment modalities. Western approaches and the Oriental approaches are considered to be complementary within the framework of a holistic and integrative therapeutic model.

The concept of a paradigm is very holistic in nature. It has two general levels. The first is the encompassing whole - the summation of the parts. It consists of the theories, laws, rules, models, concepts, and definitions that go into a generally accepted fundamental theory of science. Such a paradigm is "global" in character. The other level of paradigm is that it can also be just one of these laws, theories, models, etc. that combine to formulate a "global" paradigm. At times when a particular paradigm in use is unable to account for anomalies that appear, a revolutionary switch to a new paradigm occurs. (Polkinghorne, 1983, p. 113) The twentieth century has seen a paradigm shift toward holism in such diverse areas as politics, social thinking, psychology, management theory, and medicine. As stated earlier, these have included the practical application of Marx's thinking in Communist and Socialist states, experiments in collective living, the rise of Gestalt psychology, systems theory, and concern with the whole person in alternative medicine. All these have been reactions "against excessive individualism with its attendant alienation and fragmentation, and exhibit a commonsense appreciation of human beings' interdependency with one another and with the environment." (1976, p. 15). Holism as a systems approach uses a logic that represents a more open use of reason and shares the problem-solving goal of practical reason. This is especially helpful in understanding the autism diagnosis, and can provide the support most parents (such as myself) would need in important areas of their child's life. For example, a study by Newsome (2000) found that parental perceptions of support suggest that social workers should have more contact with families during the transitional phase, and that families would welcome this support.

Based on an examination of past and current policy provisions concerning autism, a number of problems have arisen in regards to social work involvement and intervention. Due to the nature of autism only recently hitting the headlines and striking awareness, social workers and other educational professionals need to be trained to understand the disorder and its severity. In 1989, Munoz made the case that personnel preparation in the field of autism had been inadequate. Her admonition is no less accurate today. This is true not only of social workers, but teachers, school psychologist, residential care workers, family counselors, and other professionals could benefit from intensive pre-service and in-service training on autism. State programming policies also must be implemented fully in order that proposed interventions meet local needs and convictions (Moroz, 1989). Furthermore, social workers can be in the forefront of community education which also is needed to increase awareness of autism. Such efforts could generate support for the development and awareness of services in most communities. What is more, they will be helpful to families to cope with their autistic child's behaviors with understanding and without judgment. In conclusion, social workers must continue to actively support families on early intervention and preschool teams, where they collaboratively can help families coordinate the complex array of services that families encounter during this transition stage. Parents need the best information about autism possible, and they need support from professionals in order to understand and navigate this disorder. Training sessions where professionals and parents learn to collaborate is essential for the bio-psycho-social well being of the child with autism. This holistic paradigm of social work contributes to understanding the dynamic web and interconnectedness of autism and offers hope that changes can occur at any level by understanding the inter communication and interrelatedness of its parts.

CHAPTER 3:

BIOLOGICAL ASPECTS

What causes autism specifically is not known. Some experts believe the cause is biochemical. It is thought to be biological in that it is four times more prevalent in boys than girls. But regardless of gender, autism is known to interfere with the normal development of the brain in the areas of reasoning, social interaction and communication skills. Children and adults with autism typically have deficiencies in verbal and non-verbal communication, social interactions and leisure or play activities. The disorder makes it hard for them to communicate with others and relate to the outside world. They may exhibit repeated body movements (hand flapping, rocking), unusual responses to people or attachments to objects, and resist any changes in routines. In some cases, aggressive and/or self-injurious behavior may be present.

There are no diagnostic medical tests. A diagnosis is mainly based on observations of the child's communication, behavior and developmental levels. However, because many of the behaviors associated with autism are shared by other disorders, a medical doctor may complete various medical tests to rule out other possible causes. Because autism is a spectrum disorder, no one method alone is usually effective in treating it. Professionals and families have found that a combination of treatments may be valuable in treating symptoms and behaviors that make it hard for individuals with autism to function. These may include a combination of psychosocial and pharmacological interventions. Although prescribing medications is beyond the purview of social workers, it is important that they become familiar with their purposes and possible side effects. Aman et al.(2003) report in their research that the most commonly prescribed drugs were the antidepressants (fluoxetine, sertraline, fluvoxamine), followed by the neuroleptics (risperidone, olanzapine, thioridazine), antiepileptics (valproicacid, carbamazapine, lamotrigine), antihypertensives (clonidine, propanolol, metoprolol), stimulants (methylphenidate, dextroamphetamine, amphetamine salts), sedative/anxiolytics (melatonin, buspirone, diazepam), and mood stabilizers (valproic acid, carbamazepam, lithium, and others). Forty-five percent of individuals were on one agent and 20% were on two or more psychotropic agents.

Compared with a study 8 to 10 years ago (Aman, Van Bourgondien, Wolford, & Sarphare, 1995), there has been a substantial increase in the use of the SSRIs (266%), antihypertensives (200%), and stimulants (43%). Autism supplements (B6, dimethylglycine, dimethylaminoethanol) have increased by one hundred percent. The investigators highlight limitations in the empirical basis for much of this treatment and the need for research to address these issues and others that affect effective pharmacological treatment. Social workers, for example, frequently deal with compliance issues in the administration of these medications to children, and the parents' acceptance of the need for their child to take these medications.

Biological and Environmental View:

Those who hold true to a biological and environmental view see autism is a biological disorder with psychological and behavioral symptoms. Many different theories fall within the biological view of autism, ranging from genetics to different brain anatomy to viral infection. What biological researchers all have in common is the belief that autism is caused by something in the child's biological make-up and that the psychological and behavioral symptoms are a result of the child's biology. Biological interventions are based on changing the child's physiology, either through medication, diet, or targeting physiological systems such as auditory processing. The environmental view, however, holds that while genetics play an important role in autism, the emphasis should be placed on environmental influences that trigger the expression of genes. According to an environmentalist, a child may be born with a predisposition to autism, but for the disorder to become expressed, the child must come into contact with an environmental agent to which the child has an increased sensitivity. In designing an intervention, environmental researchers would look to eliminate the environmental factors that could trigger the expression of autism. For example, Changes to diet and the addition of certain vitamins or minerals may also help with behavioral issues. According to the Autism Society of America (2004), over the past 10 years, there have been claims that adding essential vitamins such as B6 and B12 and removing gluten and casein from a child's diet may improve digestion, allergies and sociability. The following is a list of multiple therapies, treatments – both statistically documented in peer reviewed journals and experimental – that hold true to this biological and environmental thought. Many of these therapies have been in practice over the last 10-15 years, when Autism started to become more widely researched (www.reveloutionhealth.com, 2007). To discuss each and every one here specifically would require a book in of itself, so I suggest doing an internet research on the topic that interests you most:

- Alpha Lipoic Acid (ALA)
- Ambrotose Complex etc. (Arabinogalactan Formulas)
- Applied Behavior Analysis: Lovaas Therapy
- Applied Behavior Analysis: Picture Exchange Communication Systems (PECS)
- Applied Behavior Analysis: Pivotal Response Treatment (PRT)
- Applied Behavior Analysis: Reciprocal Imitation
- Applied Behavior Analysis: Verbal Behavior
- Aricept
- Aromatherapy etc. (Essential Oils)
- Autism Summer Camps
- Bach Flower Remedies (Flower Essences)
- Bentonite Clay (Montmorillonite)
- Bodywork Therapies: CranioSacral Therapy
- Bodywork Therapies: Shiatsu Pressure Point Massage
- Bodywork Therapies: Therapeutic Massage

- Bodywork Therapies: Trigger Point / Myofascial Therapy
- Bu Spar
- Calcium
- Calcium; Magnesium Formulas
- Catapres
- Celexa
- Chelation Therapy: DMPS
- Chelation Therapy: DMSA; ALA
- Chemet
- Chemical Avoidance
- Chinese Herbal Medicine
- Chiropractic Therapy
- Cod Liver Oil
- Colostrum
- Creative Arts Therapy: Drama Therapy
- Creative Arts Therapy: Music Therapy
- Dental Procedures: Mercury Amalgam Filling Removal
- Desyrel
- Diet: Candida Reduction
- Diet: Feingold Diet etc. (Avoiding Food Additives)
- Diet: Gluten-free
- Diet: Gluten-Free; Casein-Free (GFCF)
- Diet: Lactose-free

- Diet: Specific Carbohydrate Diet (SCD)
- Dilantin
- Dimethylglycine (DMG)
- Docosahexaenoic Acid (DHA)
- EASe CD etc. (Electronic Auditory Stimulation)
- Education: Special Needs Education
- Effexor
- Enzyme Formulas (Digestive)
- Exercise: Aerobics
- Fiber Supplements: Metamucil etc. (Psyllium)
- Fish Oil
- Flax Seed Oil (Omega-3 Alpha-Linolenic Acid)
- Folic Acid
- Fresh Water Algae
- GABA (Gamma-Aminobutyric Acid)
- Gabitril
- Geodon
- Homeopathy (Homeopathic Formulas)
- Hyperbaric Oxygen Treatment (HBOT)
- Klonopin
- L-Carnitine (Carnitine)
- L-Carnosine (Carnosine)
- L-Glutamine (Glutamine)

- L-Glutathione (Glutathione)
- L-Taurine (Taurine)
- Lamictal
- Lithobid
- Luvox
- Magnesium
- Magnetic Therapy: Static Magnetic Fields
- Melatonin
- Methylphenidate
- Multi-Vitamin; Mineral Supplements (combined)
- Neurontin
- Nutritional Supplement Formulas: Antioxidant Formulas
- Occupational Therapy: Auditory Integration Therapy
- Occupational Therapy: Neurodevelopmental Therapy (NDT)
- Occupational Therapy: Sensory Integration Therapy
- Olive Leaf Extract
- Patient Education: Books, Magazines, Newsletters
- Patient Education: Email Newsletters
- Paxil
- Physical Therapy: Brain Gym
- Prayer / Spirituality
- Probiotics (Lactobacillus, Bifidobacterium etc.)
- Prozac

- Remeron
- Risperdal
- Risperdal Consta
- Risperidone
- Secretin
- Selenium
- Serenity etc. (Lithium Orotate)
- Seroquel
- Soy Supplements (Capsules / Powder)
- Speech-Language Therapy: Earobics
- Speech-Language Therapy: Fast ForWord
- Speech-Language Therapy: Sign Language
- Speech-Language Therapy: Speech Therapy
- Strattera
- Teaching Methods: Direct Skill Instruction
- Teaching Methods: Floor Time
- Teaching Methods: Rapid Prompting Method (RPM)
- Teaching Methods: Relationship Development Intervention (RDI) Program
- Teaching Methods: Social Stories
- Teaching Methods: Son-Rise Program
- Teaching Methods: TEACCH
- Teaching Methods: Video / In-vivo Modeling

- Tegretol
- Tenex
- Tofranil
- Topamax
- Transfer Factors
- Trileptal
- Tryptophan (L-Tryptophan)
- Valtrex
- Vision Therapy: Visual Exercises
- Visual Aid Products: Irlen Lenses
- Vitamin A
- Vitamin B-12 (Injections)
- Wellbutrin
- Yoga
- Zinc
- Zoloft

Not all researchers and experts agree about whether these therapies are effective or scientifically valid. Clearly, further research is needed.

The Vaccine Controversy:

It has been hypothesized that the Measles/Mumps/ Rubella (MMR) vaccine caused autism in children. Many parents report that their children were "normal" until they received the MMR vaccine. Then, after getting the vaccine, the children started showing symptoms of autism. Because the symptoms of autism begin to occur around the same time as the child's MMR vaccination, parents and families view the vaccine as the cause of the autism. These parents' beliefs and observations were reinforced by a small study of bowel disease and autism, published by Wakefield and his colleagues in 1998 (Wakefield et al 1998). The study's authors suggested that there was a link between the MMR vaccine and autism. However, the study did not include scientific testing to find out if there was a link. According to the CDC (2007) The authors relied on the reports of parents and families of the 12 children with autism involved in the study to make their suggestion and did not provide scientific proof that there was any link.

Since this study was published in 1998, a number of other studies have also been published that suggested a link between the MMR vaccine and autism (Singh et al 1998; Horvath et al 1999; O'Leary et al 2000; Wakefield et al 2000; Kawashima et al 2000), but to date there is no definite, scientific data showing a direct link of any vaccine or combination of vaccines can cause autism. The table below cites current CDC studies on the Vaccines and ASD. One in particular, the Thimerosal Screening Study (2003) showed a link between Thimerosal and Tics, which reinforces the possibility of a link between the MMR vaccine and ASD.

TABLE 1 - CDC STUDIES ON VACCINES AND AUTISM SPECTRUM DISORDERS (CDC, 207)

November 2002

Denmark Measles-Mumps-Rubella (MMR)/Autism Study

CDC has an ongoing cooperative agreement with the Danish Medical Research Council. This agreement supports collaboration with Danish researchers and gives CDC an opportunity to pursue causes of birth defects and developmental disabilities through Denmark's unique public health data infrastructure. The Danish study, which followed more than 500,000 children for 7 years, found no association between the MMR vaccination and autism. The results were published in the *New England Journal of Medicine* (2002;347:1477-82)

Thimerosal Screening Study

November 2003

The Vaccine Safety Datalink (VSD) was used to screen for possible associations between exposure to vaccines containing thimerosal and a variety of renal, neurologic, and developmental problems. In the first phase of this study, CDC used data from the two VSD managed care organizations (MCOs) with automated outpatient data (where more subtle effects of mercury toxicity might be seen). The CDC and VSD researchers found statistically significant associations between thimerosal and two neurodevelopmental disorders—language delays and tics. However, the associations were weak and were not consistent between the two MCOs. No association was shown with autism. In the second phase of the study, CDC researchers looked at data from a third MCO with similar automated vaccination and outpatient data to see if these findings could be repeated. Analyses using the same methods as in the first two MCOs did not confirm results seen in the first phase. The results were published in *Pediatrics* (2003;112:1039-48).

Age at First MMR Vaccination in Children With Autism and School Matched Control Subjects: A Population-Based Study in Metropolitan Atlanta.

February 2004

CDC did a vaccine study as part of the Metropolitan Atlanta Developmental Disabilities Surveillance Program. The study compared the age at which children with an ASD got the Measles Mumps Rubella (MMR) vaccine with the age at which children who do not have an ASD got the vaccine. The study's results showed that children with autism received their first MMR vaccination at similar ages as children without autism. The study was published in *Pediatrics* (Feb 2004; 113(2):259-66).

The Autism and Biopsy Study

June 2007

This study is investigating whether the MMR vaccine may cause autism by a mechanism involving persistent measles virus infection in the intestine. Researchers are examining the intestinal tissue of children with autism for the presence of measles virus.

Immunizations and Possible Developmental Regression, CDC is working with the National Institutes of Health on a study to evaluate whether the MMR vaccine is linked with developmental regression, which occurs in a subset of children with autism.

Italy Thimerosal NDD Study

November 2002

CDC is collaborating with researchers in Italy to evaluate children who were randomly exposed to differing amounts of thimerosal during infancy as part of a clinical trial of whooping cough vaccines, including thimerosal-containing and thimerosal-free vaccine preparations.

Brain Studies:

According to Lee (2003) Early Autopsy research revealed a wide variety of neurological differences and damage in the brains of individuals with Autism, rather than finding a single biological brain disorder. More recent detailed microscopic forensic studies have revealed several features that can be identified in significant numbers of people with Autism, but not all people with Autism. This supports the proposal that Autism is really a set of biological subgroups with a variety of neurological conditions that create similar symptoms. Some of the structural and functional features that have been found across subgroups of people with Autism, which can be directly related are:

- ➢ Changes in the size and thickness of the Cerebral Cortex.
- ➢ Changes in the neural fibers of the Corpus Callosum:
- ➢ Changes in the functional activity of the Front Lobes
- ➢ Changes in the functional activity of the Temporal Lobes:
  Changes in the structure of functional activity of the Limbic System:
- ➢ Changes in the structures and functional activities of the Thalamus which controls processing of sensory input--except smell, the Hypothalamus which produces and regulates motivation and emotion, and the Hippocampus and Amygdala which helps manage Information processing and integration in ways that effects behavior. All of these are shown to be involved in Autism.

These emergent biomedical findings mean that developmental systems science approach to research may soon become of critical interest to the Autism community. New medical technologies combined with the current scientific interest in how the body and brain interact and how genetic and environmental influences operate could yield new and important information about Autism. Other researchers in the field of applied behavior analysis through Cure Autism Now Foundation are investigating the possibility that under certain conditions, a cluster of unstable genes may interfere with brain development resulting in autism. Still other medical researchers through the Mt. Sinai Sever Institute for Autism and the University of Toronto are investigating problems during pregnancy or delivery as well as environmental factors such as viral infections, metabolic imbalances, and exposure to environmental chemicals. All in all, medical researchers are continuing to explore different explanations for the various forms of autism and how it impacts on the current thinking in regards to the individual with the Autistic diagnosis.

CHAPTER 4:

PAST AND PRESENT POLICIES

Historically, governmental policy surrounding Autism has been one of insitutionalization. Ninety-five percent of persons with autism lived in institutions because of lack of alternative educational and human services, at least until 1976. (Moroz, p.113) As a group, children and youths with autism are the population most at risk in the United States for institutionalization due to their specific behaviors. Most children and adults with autism received their primary education and needs in institutions until the early 1970's, when deinsutionalization and the increase in availability of psychiatric medications took effect. Prior to that, persons with severe and persistent mental disorders were generally cared for in state hospitals. (Grob, 1993) If admitted in their youth, as with many autistics, they often remained institutionalized for decades. After 1970, the mentally disabled's care came under the jurisdiction of a series of federal entitlement programs, which presumed that income payments would enable persons to live in the community. With the autistic population, however, most were moved into community residences, developmental centers, or returned home. The guiding theory of the deinstitutionalization of the developmentally disabled population became that of integration and normalization. An example of this is the Willowbrook

Decree of New York State. Former Governor Hugh L. Carey signed this decree in 1975 to "Provide safe, attractive, comfortable and homelike environments in which more personalized care is delivered to the severely mentally disabled and retarded (CQC, 1982.) This decree grew out of strong convictions about the negative qualities of large segregated, custodial institutions and the right of the disabled individual to grow and develop as members of their own community. In New York State, the care of the Autistic and Developmentally Disabled was then put into the care of the New York State Office of Mental Retardation and Developmental Disabilities. Many mentally disabled individuals, through this office, were then placed into the community into care facilities, conversely to save the Federal and State Government money. In a 1979 study of facilities in New York, the estimated yearly costs of institutional care to be $14,700 annually, compared with $9300 - $11,000 annually for group home care (Spano, 1987.) In 1982, the average annual cost per resident in a community residence increased to $28,639 annually, compared to an annual per client cost of $37,024 per client in a Developmental Center or an institution. (CQC, 1982) For those that lived at home, Federal entitlements, such as Supplemental Security Income (SSI), food stamps, and Medicaid helped defray the costs of living at home. Currently, a Developmentally Disabled child diagnosed as autistic is eligible for SSI payments of up to $469.00 per month plus Medicaid benefits, and adults about $565.00 per month. However, the autistic individual is not classified into its own sub-category. According to the Social Security Administration, if the autistic individual has an IQ of under 75, they are classified as mentally retarded. If over 75, they are considered emotionally disturbed or other mental disorders (SSA-1997). The mentally retarded classification, therefore, would affect approximately 75% of the autistic population. These two categories compromise 27.8% and 29.9% of the population, respectively.

While no one can predict the future, we do know that some adults with autism live and work independently in the community, while others depend on the support of family and professionals. Adults with autism can benefit from vocational training to provide them with the skills needed for obtaining jobs, in addition to social and recreational programs. Recently, many individuals with Asperger's or HFA are now attending college, confounding educators in a /university setting in how to handle these students and provide them with the necessary accommodations to help them with their educational journey. Furthermore, adults with autism may live in a variety of residential settings, ranging from independent home or apartments to group homes, supervised apartment settings, living with other family members to more structured residential care.

Educational Policy:

In addition to the deinstitutionalization of the autistic and mentally disabled population came the need for abundant and appropriate educational placement. Historically, disabled (and autistic) children were removed from regular classrooms and placed in special classes, home teaching, private schools or institutions. However, with the movement towards deinstitutionalization, there became a need for more special education programs in a time where they were few around and waiting lists for others. For Example, in New York State (a progressive state in special education services) a 1944 law declared that the Education Department should "stimulate all private and public efforts designed to relieve, care for, cure or educate physically handicapped children," and coordinate its efforts with other governmental programs. This policy statement was extended in 1957 to include mentally retarded children as well. Ten years later the "handicapped child" was legally, and more flexibly, redefined as an individual who "because of mental, physical or emotional reasons, cannot be educated in regular classes but can benefit by special services and programs." (Data Research, 1997) This definition summarized New York State policy, which since the early years of the century had favored removing handicapped children from regular classrooms and schools, and placing them in "special classes," home teaching, or private schools.

In the 1950s and '60s this policy began to shift toward "inclusion." Public schools were authorized to hold special classes for severely mentally handicapped children starting 1955, and required to do so after 1961. During the 1960s the New York State Department of Education encouraged efforts to place multi-handicapped or brain-injured children in public schools. Special aid to schools for education of handicapped children, abolished in 1962, was restored by legislative acts in 1974 and 1976. A broad-ranging Regents policy statement on "Education of Children with Handicapping Conditions" in 1973 recommended placing them in regular classrooms when possible. School committees on the handicapped were required by a Commissioner's regulation. In 1977 the Commissioner ordered the New York City school system to improve its special education programs, which had long waiting lists and many underserved children. Federal aid for new programs to educate children with handicapping conditions was authorized under the ESEA Title VI-A in 1967. Congress passed the Education of All Handicapped Children Act in 1975 (revised in 1990 and again in 1997 as the Individuals with Disabilities Education Act, IDEA). This federal act required the states to provide all children with disabilities with a "free, appropriate education in the least restrictive environment. However, minimal federal aid (about 9% of all funding) came with this big mandate. Therefore the state and the local governments were required to pick up the other 91% of the tab. A 1976 state law required the school committees on special education to develop an individualized educational program in the "least restrictive environment, After the mid-1970s, most New York State school districts were responsible for recommending and providing services for all children of school age who were identified as having disabilities.

Parental Involvement in Education:

A method under the IDEA to involve parents in their child's educational plan is the development of the Individualized Educational Program (IEP). The IEP is the cornerstone for the education of a child with a disability. The IEP is a written statement of a child's educational program, which identifies the services a child needs so that he or she may grow and learn during the school year. The IEP outlines the child's special education plan by defining goals for the school year, services needed to help the child meet those goals, and a method of evaluating the student's progress. As its name suggests, the Individualized Educational Program should be written to reflect the child's individual and unique needs. Accordingly, no single IEP would be appropriate for all children with autism. Under explicit provisions of P.L. 105-17 which are effective July 1st 1998, Parents must be included in the IEP team (Sec. 614 (d)(1)(B)). Additionally with the 1997 Reauthorization of IDEA, parents must now be included as "members of any group that makes decisions on the educational placement of the child" (Sec. 614 (f)). Parents may bring a list of suggested goals and objectives, as well as additional information that may be pertinent, to the IEP meeting.

Under the IEDA Section PL 94-142, Autism was categorized as a "severe emotional disturbance." Although this was eventually changed at the federal level to a subcategory under other health impaired in 1981, autism still was categorized as an emotional disturbance for educational purposes in many parts of the U.S. (Moroz, p.108). It wasn't until 1990 that the IDEA, under its revisions, saw autism as a separate and distinct category. Therefore, much data relating to the education and service of autistic children is limited to only a few years. According to the US Department of Education Statistics (2002) New York State has a 202% increase from 1992 to 2001 in the amount of children that were classified with "autism". The significant increase is due, in part, to the new research and increased awareness to the autistic diagnosis.

Educational Management:

For most autistic children, educational management should emphasize development of social skills and communicative language. The long-term goal should be to permit the child to function as effectively and comfortably as possible in the least restrictive environment. (Bauer, 1993) But the majority of autistic children in special education classrooms are unable to move into "less restrictive environments" due to their disruptive behaviors. This is due, in part, to the education of professions about autism – which has been reportedly slow but has improved over the last decade due to increased awareness. As stated earlier, autistic children were clumped together with children with "serious emotional disturbances." Most public school teachers in the field of autism, according to Munoz, had received training in emotional disturbances, learning disabilities, behavior disorders, or some other category of students less severely impaired than children with autism (p. 113.) Many teachers also reported feeling poorly prepared to work with the autistic children in the classroom. In New York City, for example, children with autism are grouped under an "Autistic" category and are regulated to a specialized Instructional Environment (SIE – III) – segregated from the mainstream population. Autistic children in the SIE-III units are in a classroom of a 6:1:1 student-teacher ratio, with individualized support services of speech, occupational, and physical therapy as deemed appropriate. However, due to lack of training with this population, the teachers use a curriculum focused on "life skills" and little to no intervention for their maladaptive or disruptive behaviors. Furthermore, the autistic child in this SIE-III unit is restricted from the chance of being integrated into a less restrictive environment by physically being separated from regular or higher functioning disabled children.

Therapeutic Educational Programs:

There are many different types of therapeutic programs offered in private school and therapeutic settings. One of the most effective programs proven to work effectively according to documented research is the statewide program in North Carolina, developed by Dr. Eric Schloper, Dr. Meisbov, and associates at division TEACCH at the University of North Carolina. The longitudinal study of early intensive behavioral treatment of autistic children by Dr. O. Ivar Lovaas in California is the second. What are the cost benefits to each of these programs, compared to the traditional methods used at present? It is important to examine and compare each program specifically to its teaching method, success rate, and monetary cost to run it. It is also important to examine the in-tangential benefits that come with each program (e.g.: an autistic individual possibly becoming a productive member in society) and measure the benefits of each program to the movement of the autistic child.

Applied Behavior Analysis:

The first program that I will discuss is the Lovaas style Intensive behavioral treatment program founded by Dr. O. Ivar Lovaas from the University of

California, Loss Angeles. It is argued (Lovaas, 1979) that behavior modification is the most effective form of intervention in the treatment of autism. Applied Behavior Analysis (ABA) is a science, which seeks to use empirically validated behavior change procedures for assisting individuals in developing skills with social value. The procedures used in intensive behavioral intervention programs for children with autism are drawn primarily from the rich base of research generated by practitioners of ABA. The constellation of procedures typically includes use of "discrete trial instruction" but is not limited to that method of instruction. Terms, which denote the comprehensiveness of the intervention, include intensive behavioral intervention (IBI), behavioral therapy, and behavioral treatment. This method focuses on the elimination of the many maladaptive behaviors demonstrated by autistic children. It also includes the broadening the behavioral repertoire to include more adaptive patterns of behavior (Waters, 1990) The various procedures employed to increase behavior are generally based on the operant principles of reinforcement for desires behavior while maladaptive behaviors can be decreased through the use on consequences. This viewpoint is based on the idea that the different autistic behaviors might be related to several different kinds of antecedent conditions. One characteristic of autistic children is that they express little emotion. These behaviors are, it is argued (Lovaas, 1979), left largely unaltered because they are not well understood and therefore not taught. The Lovaas model is notable because of the striking results that are claimed for it, including increase in IQ, educational placement, and adaptive function.

The initial Lovaas treatment program started with young children under four years of age, lasted two years, and was very intensive – requiring one to one staff: child ratio 40 hours per week. The children were then followed over a 5 to 10 year period, which resulted in over 60% of the children either being in less restrictive or general educational settings. The other 40% were in special education settings, but only 15% of those made no significant gains. (Bauer, 1995)   For example, a single varied study conducted by Ogletree, Fischer, and Sprouse (1995) focused on an intensive Lovaas-style behavioral treatment plan to stimulate sematic/pragmatic language development in a child with high functioning autism. The independent variable was a treatment sequence emphasizing video vignettes and role-plays. Dependent variables included efficient gaze, responding without delays and topic maintained.   The study was done over 12 treatment sessions of 45 minutes each twice per week. The results of the study showed a 61% increase in appropriate gaze, a marked increase in topic episodes of appropriate conversational length (47%) but no change in the responses without delays from the baseline sessions. (Ogletree, ET al, 1995) Behavior change through the use of behavior modification is sometimes very slow. Lovaas (1979) commented on the fact that it is hard work to treat autistic people because of the slow rate of response to treatment. This style of behavior modification requires long periods of intensive work, early intervention (pre-school age), and intensive training in order to be successful.

Since this therapy has had numerous research articles with clear empirical data supporting it, the New York State Board of Education, or example, took a logical positivism approach to the acceptance of this method of teaching and has published a series of Clinical Practice Guidelines: ABA, or Applied Behavior Analysis, is the only scientifically validated treatment for autism in early to middle childhood. This claim, as per Dr. Bernard Rimland, explicitly reject other vitamin therapy, gluten-and casein-free diets, anti-fungal treatment, auditory integration training, sensory integration, and many other interventions which employ more of an empirical viewpoint, or "experience knowledge" formulated by mainly by parents and other professionals in the treatment of the autistic child.

The rival claim to this is that, while ABA therapy is a solid approach, "parents have a right and an obligation to consider all possible forms of intervention, including those which may not yet have won the stamp of approval of whatever person or committee feels qualified to pass judgment on candidate interventions." (Rimland, 2002 Para 12) Although there are statically proven counter claims to the ABA theory, skepticism has enabled for many individuals to take a semi-postpostivist viewpoint in the treatment of the autistic child. While embracing the ABA theory, many parents look to other accepted forms of therapies, such as sensory integration therapy, to supplement their child's improvement.

TEACCH:

Developed in the early 1970's by Dr. Eric Schopler, the TEACCH (Treatment and Education of Autistic and related Communication Handicapped Children) approach includes a focus on the person with autism and the development of a program around this person's skills, interests, and needs. The major priorities include centering on the individual, understanding autism, adopting appropriate adaptations, and a broadly based intervention strategy building on existing skills and interests. (Meisbov, 1994) By focusing on the individual the person or autistic child becomes the priority, rather than any philosophical notion like inclusion, discrete trial training, facilitated communication, etc. An individualized assessment plan is created to understand the individual better and also "the culture of autism," suggesting that people with autism are part of a distinctive group with common characteristics that are different, but not necessarily inferior, to the rest of society. Emphasizing assessment and the culture of autism requires an understanding of people with autism as they are and to build programs around where each person is functioning.

Structured teaching is an important priority because of the TEACCH research and experience that structure fits the "culture of autism" more effectively. Organizing the physical environment (if by colors, numbers, or other visual cues), developing schedules and work systems, making expectations clear and explicit, and using visual materials have been some effective ways of developing skills and allowing people with autism to use these skills independently of direct adult prompting (as with the Lovaas style program) and cueing. Most programs dealing with developmental disabilities emphasize remediating deficits and focus their entire efforts on that goal. The

TEACCH approach, respecting the "culture of autism," recognized that the differences between people with autism and others. (Meisbov, 1994) Their relative strengths in visual skills, recognizing details, and memory, among other areas, can become the basis of successful adult functioning.

The TEACCH approach is also broad-based, taking into account all aspects of the lives of people with autism and their families. Although independent work skills are emphasized, it is also recognized that "life is not all work and that communication, social and leisure skills can be learned by people with autism and can have an important impact on their well-being" (Bauer, 1995.) An important part of the TEACCH curriculum is developing communication skills, pursuing social and leisure interests, and encouraging people with autism to pursue more of these opportunities. In addition to these techniques of understanding autism, developing appropriate structures, promoting independent work skills, emphasizing strengths and interests and fostering communication, social and leisure outlets, the TEACCH approach is most successfully implemented on a systems level. Based on the concept that coordination and integration over time is as important as consistency within a given situation, the TEACCH approach is most effective when it is applied across age groups and agencies. TEACCH believes that the interests of people with autism are best served with coordinated and cooperative programming based on consistent principles over a lifetime. The TEACCH assessment called PEP (Psycho Educational Profile) tries to identify areas where the person "passes", areas where the skill isn't there yet, and areas where the skill is emerging. These domains are then put in an education program for the person. Several outcome studies have examined parent reports of the effectiveness of Structured Teaching and the TEACCH intervention programs Schopler, Meisbov, DeVellis, and Short (1981) received completed questionnaires from 348 families who had participated in the TEACCH program. Parents consistently and with overwhelming enthusiasm, reported that their relationships with Division TEACCH were positive, productive, and enriching. Most impressive were the parents' reports of the high percentage of their adolescent and adult children with autism who were still functioning in community-based programs. Of the families with older children among the respondents, 96% reported that their children were still living in their local communities. This response compared favorably with concurrent follow-up studies showing that between 39% and 74% of autistic adolescents and adults were generally in large residential programs outside of their local communities. The number of clients successfully working in the TEACCH Supported Employment Program is another important outcome measure, perhaps even the most important because it represents the culmination of TEACCH's many intervention activities, early identification, parent training, education, social and leisure skill development, communication training, and vocational preparation. Successful Supported Employment placements are a major goal of many programs serving people with autism and related disabilities. Division TEACCH is using three models of supported Employment: individual competitive placements, dispersed enclaves, and mobile crews. All of these models have clients working a minimum of 15 hours per week earning minimum wage or above with an adult to client supervision ratio of 3:1 or less intensive Supported employment clients earn an average hourly wage of $5.30 working an average if 28 hours per week.

CHAPTER 5:

SOCIAL ASPECTS OF AUTISM

As described by Kettner and Moroney (1999) a social situation is a problem when it becomes a "source of distress" (p. 34) The Social problem of Autism extends beyond the affected child or adult, and to those who care for them. Caring for an Autistic child can be overwhelming and sometimes overly impossible due to the specific behaviors that those children exhibit. Respite care is often difficult if not impossible to obtain, let alone a qualified worker to handle the child's behaviors. Furthermore, there are still so many families who are not familiar with the variety of services and resources available to them. When they are in urgent or immediate need, there are few options available to them. This is especially true in the care of a consumer with a Diagnosis of Autism and their families, where "Autism" resources are limited and guidance of a professional such as a psychologist or social worker can be crucial. Helping autistic children and their families achieve a sense of belonging in their community are generally not addressed by experts in the field. For example, a single parent raising a child with Autism experiences the same range of reactions and need that couples do. Coping, however, may be considerably harder, because the single parent must make important decisions alone. A child with autism obviously puts a great deal of stress on any relationship. Sometimes a marriage, already teetering, will topple under the weight of the extra stress. When this happens, one parent – usually the mother

– is left with the major responsibility for raising the child with autism. This chapter will examine the social impact of autism on the affected child and the family, and attempt to provide some suggestions to address this issue.

As mentioned in chapter one, autism is known to interfere with the normal development of the brain in the areas of reasoning, social interaction and communication skills. Children and adults with autism typically have deficiencies in verbal and non-verbal communication, social interactions and leisure or play activities. The disorder makes it hard for them to communicate with others and relate to the outside world. They may exhibit repeated body movements (hand flapping, rocking), unusual responses to people or attachments to objects and resist any changes in routines. In some cases, aggressive and/or self-injurious behavior may be present. There are great differences among people with autism. Some individuals mildly affected may exhibit only slight delays in language and greater challenges with social interactions. They may have average or above average verbal, memory or spatial skills but find it difficult to be imaginative or join in a game of softball with their friends. Others more severely affected may need greater assistance in handling day to day activities like crossing the street or making a purchase, putting more stress and responsibility upon the parent and/or caregiver. While no one can predict the future, we do know that some adults with autism live and work independently in the community, while others depend on the support of family and professionals. Studies show that adults with autism can benefit from vocational training to provide them with the skills needed for obtaining jobs, in addition to social and recreational programs. Adults with autism are known to live in a variety of residential settings, ranging from independent home or apartments to group homes, supervised apartment settings, living with other family members to more structured residential care.

Quality of life issues for children with autism and their families can be understood by Maslow's hierarchy of needs. An example of how Maslow's hierarchal framework can be applied is by looking at the different classifications that he utilizes: survival, security, and sense of belonging, self-esteem, and self-actualization. The medical and the current psychological research have made great strides over the last 10 years in the survival and security of autistic children and their families. However, the higher level needs such as helping the autistic child and their family achieve a sense of belonging in their community for example – is still developing and perceived, as a great unmet need for the autism family.

Lack of Advancement in Educational Management:

As mentioned in the previous chapter, educational management should emphasize development of social skills and communicative language. The long-term goal should be to permit the child to function as effectively and comfortably as possible in the least restrictive environment. (Bauer, 1993) However the majority of autistic children in special education classrooms are unable to move into "less restrictive environments" due to their disruptive behaviors. This is due, in part, to the education of professions about autism –

77

which has been reportedly slow. As stated earlier, autistic children were clumped together with children with "serious emotional disturbances." Most public school teachers in the field of autism, according to Munoz, have received training in emotional disturbances, learning disabilities, behavior disorders, or some other category of students less severely impaired than children with autism (p. 113.) Many parents and teachers also reported feeling poorly prepared to work with the autistic children in the classroom and at home. In New York City, for example, children with autism are grouped under an "Autistic" category and are regulated to a specialized Instructional Environment (SIE – III) – segregated from the mainstream population. Autistic children in the SIE-III units are in a classroom of a 6:1:1 student-teacher ratio, with individualized support services of speech, occupational, and physical therapy as deemed appropriate. However, due to lack of training with this population, the teachers use a curriculum focused on "life skills" and little to no intervention for their maladaptive or disruptive behaviors. Many treatment or behavioral plans are not carried over into the home due the lack of education by the parent or the support they receive from the school. Furthermore, the autistic child in this SIE-III unit is restricted from the chance of being integrated into a less restrictive environment by physically being separated from regular or higher functioning disabled children.

Stereotypes of the Autistic Individual in Society:

At first glance, the person with autism may appear to have mental retardation, a behavior disorder, or even problems with hearing. Many feel that a person with autism is in fact, mentally retarded or, in the case of a high-functioning autistic, and individual with schizophrenia. For example, individuals with autism have been seen taking a stranger's food right off their plate. As a result of these potential experiences, families often feel uncomfortable taking their child to the homes of friends or relatives. This makes holidays an especially difficult time for these families. Feeling like they cannot socialize or relate to others, parents of children with autism may experience a sense of isolation from their friends, relatives and community.

Inadequate Attention to Support Services to Families:

Research indicates that parents of children with autism experience greater stress than parents of children with mental retardation and Down syndrome (Powers, 1989). This may be a result of the distinct characteristics that individuals with autism exhibit. An individual with autism may not be able to express their basic wants or needs. Therefore, parents are left playing a guessing game. A child's deficits in social skills, such as the lack of appropriate play, are also stressful for families. Individuals lacking appropriate leisure skills often require constant structure of their time, a task not feasible to accomplish in the home environment. Furthermore, many families struggle with the additional challenges of getting their child to sleep through the night or eat a wider variety of foods. All of these deficits and behaviors are physically exhausting for families and emotionally draining. Taking an individual with autism out into the community can be a source of stress for parents. People may stare, make comments or fail to understand any of the odd behaviors that may occur. Lastly, Parents of children with autism are grieving the loss of the "typical" child that they expected to have. In addition, parents are grieving the loss of lifestyle that they expected for themselves and family. The feelings of grief that parents experience can be a source of stress due its ongoing nature. When the needs of the family are being considered, more attention is being placed on the Autistic child and the "need" for the family to devote their time to managing the child's educational plan, while ignoring the need of the parent or caregiver.

Possible Solutions:

In extrapolations from the many identified normative, perceived, expressed and relative needs of the social problem of Autism, it may be feasible therefore to identify the following for possible objectives towards a solution:

1.) Education of Teachers and School Personnel, as well as support staff is needed:

2.) Education of Medical Professionals is Needed

3.) Local and National policy changes are needed, especially on an educational level.

3.) Programmatic Changes in the Schools are needed.

4.) Family Advocacy, Education and Support programs are needed.

Of the above solutions, the one proposing the greatest need for a program is based on family education, advocacy and support programs for an intervention base. By providing increased support services that address the concrete needs and psychological as well as social needs of the autistic child and family, will lead to an overall reduction in stress level and understanding of the developmental disability, while empowering the family to cope with the autistic child. Many autistic children and their families' are often in need of support and advocacy services throughout the child's lifespan. For one, the benefits of involving parents in their children's education and overall well being are well documented and routinely practiced by school social workers. Family involvement in the education of an autistic child at school and at home becomes more critical because the child's successful development of independent living skills and the family's ability to maintain the young person at home hinges partially on the comprehensiveness and continuity of the child's education (Munoz, 1989). Due to the nature of autism only recently becoming an educational classification, teachers and other educational professionals should be trained to understand the disorder and its severity. Personnel preparation, according to Munoz (1989), in the field of autism has been inadequate. Not only with teachers, but social workers, school psychologist, residential care, family counselors, and other professionals could benefit from intensive pre-service and in-service training on autism. These additional services can help families deal with the autistic child's behaviors without judgment and understanding.

<u>After School Programs</u>:

Often, a consumer with Autism and their families are in crisis and are in need of immediate advocacy and guidance. The adult consumer with Autism historically may be rejected from one recreation program or another due to their specific individual needs and lack of social integration. This is a frequent occurrence with consumers who have Autism and their families, for the child/adult with Autism can also exhibit behaviors that can be difficult to control, and add undue stress to the caregiver. An after school program would allow the consumer and their family not to have to resort to residential placement due to lack of supports and supervision of the consumer in the home. The major priorities of an After School Program should include centering on the individual, understanding their disability and cultural background, adopting appropriate adaptations, and an intervention strategy building on existing skills and interests of the consumer. By focusing on the individual, the consumer becomes the priority. An individualized assessment plan will be created for each consumer to understand the individual better and also "the culture of autism," suggesting that people with autism are part of a distinctive group with common characteristics that are different and can be integrated to the rest of society.

Some of the recommended goals for any after school program are as follows:

1.) Behavioral/Behavioral Recreation and community integration of the consumer with daily transportation.

2.) Ability to socialize and/or learn appropriate social skills with peers in a structured and semi-structured setting.

3.) Individualized behavioral plan for the consumer developed in conjunction with the consumer's parent/caregiver. With an autistic child, the thought basis of the "perfect family" system is thrown into chaos. When one member of the family system suffers from Autism, there is a break in the communication feedback loop, creating additional stressors within the family unit. In the clinical management of the autistic child, it is important not to loose sight of the needs of the family and their input into the child's care. A supportive and educational framework is very important in helping parents cope with their child's disability and to also network with other families with autistic children as well.

Emphasizing assessment and the culture of autism requires an understanding of people with autism as they are and to build programs around where each person is functioning. An after school program should respect the "culture of autism," recognizing the differences between people with autism and others. Their relative strengths in visual skills, recognizing details, and memory, among other areas, can become the basis of successful adult functioning.

Teaching parents and the individual self-advocacy skills through workshops and group forums at the after school program site is also crucial. A behavioral evaluator should meet with the consumer's family to develop a Behavioral treatment Plan Specific to the Childs needs, and meet with the family on a monthly basis to note any progress or revisions in the plan. Once the initial needs for After School Program and Recreational Program are met, our service coordinator will continue to make the consumer/family aware of available resources and services and make appropriate referrals, including on-going service coordination if necessary. There are still so many families who are not familiar with the variety of services and resources available to them. With this service, there are two main objectives. One is to assist the family with the needs they have identified at time of referral. The second is to educate them to the various service systems that can help the consumer achieve their personal goals.

Parent/Family Training:

Parent/Family Training is a much-needed service. Often, a consumer with Autism and their families are in crisis and are in need of immediate advocacy and guidance. The adult consumer with Autism historically may be rejected from one program or another due to their specific individual needs and lack of social integration. This is a frequent occurrence with consumers who have Autism and their families, for the child/adult with Autism can also exhibit behaviors that can be difficult to control, and add undue stress to the caregiver. By providing family training for these families, we are allowing the consumer and their family not to have to resort to residential placement due to lack of supports and supervision of the consumer in the home.

There are still so many families who are not familiar with the variety of services and resources available to them. Under parent/family training, one of the goals is to assist the family with the needs they have identified at time of referral. The second is to educate them to the various service systems that can help the consumer achieve their personal goals. the major priorities of the respite program include centering on the individual, understanding their disability and cultural background, such as "the culture of autism," suggesting that people with autism are part of a distinctive group with common characteristics that are different and can be integrated to the rest of society by adopting appropriate adaptations and a intervention strategy building on existing skills and interests of the consumer. By focusing on the individual, the consumer becomes the priority.

Psycho-educational Support Group:

The support group introduces parents and family members to various behavioral procedures that have proven successful in achieving behavior changes when applied appropriately to a diverse range of skills, including toilet training, communication and interpersonal behavior skills.

Some suggested Discussion Topics that should be offered to parents should include the following:

1.) Taking care of yourself: Tips for Parents.

2.) IEPs and 504 Plans, What you might need to know.

3.) Communication w/ School Personnel about autism.

4.) Applied Behavior Analysis

5.) Visual Supports for children with autism.

6.) Sibling issues.

7.) Special Insurance Issues

8.) Dealing with Inflexibility & Difficult Moments

A sibling support group will also foster an understanding through therapeutic play, which should be lead by a skilled certified social worker or another certified professional with experience in the area of child development and autism.

Lieberman (1979) explored how self-help and support groups aid their members using a framework of change mechanisms based on Yalom's work (Lieberman et al., 1973). The results of Lieberman's (1979) comparative analyses across various self-help and professional groups indicate that a variety of helping processes are perceived to be beneficial. Consistently, the most positively perceived helping process across almost all problems is providing a new perspective through the small group process. Lieberman's analysis found similarities across all groups whether professionally led or not and whether or not they have an articulated ideology. Based on these works, the following change mechanisms are one approach to assessing self-help groups for family members of persons with serious mental illness:

- ➤ Imparting of Information (Guidance)-Peers provide information in an understandable form (Silverman, 1982). New information promotes mastery and opens possibilities for constructive life change.
- ➤ Group Cohesiveness-A sense of belonging among self-help group members with similar problems creates a feeling of cohesiveness (Lieberman, 1979). Cohesive groups offer acceptance and support for taking risks, which include sharing personal material and expressing emotions (Yalom, 1975; Lieberman, 1979). Universality-Self-help group members value an opportunity to meet others with similar problems (Gottlieb, 1982; Kagey et al., 1981; Knight et al., 1980; Levy, 1979). This is the "we-are-not-alone" phenomenon (Atwood & Williams, 1978).
- ➤ Identification-People are more influenced by those they perceive as similar to themselves. Longer-term members of the group function as role models (Suler, 1984).
- ➤ Altruism-In the process of helping others, self-help participants help themselves. The helper-therapy principle, in its simplest form, states that those who help are helped most (Riessman, 1965). Support from other group members offers an opportunity "to rehearse coping strategies and increase feelings of purpose, self-efficacy, and self worth" (Heller et al., 1997, p. 190).

> Catharsis-The accepting atmosphere of the group gives permission to ventilate resentment without fear of being criticized as a "bad parent" or an "unsympathetic spouse or sibling." The group allows expression of grief for the loss of a relative as he or she once was and for expectations that have not been fulfilled. Mourning requires a cathartic process of reviewing memories of what has been lost (Grayson, 1970).

Parents should also be taught of what is on their child's Individual Education Plan (IEP). Parents must be allowed the option of focusing on their family needs without being blamed for their child's disability. This in turn will help incorporate a sense of self-esteem by also teaching parent's self-advocacy skills through workshops and group forums and connecting them to other parent groups through. Lastly, self-actualization is the ultimate goal, helping the parent(s) or caregiver become self reliant. A supportive and educational framework is very important in helping parents cope with their child's disability and to network with other families with autistic children as well. As per Zeanah (2002) it seems that supports, appraisals, and family coping strategies are important areas of strength that may mediate stress in families of children with disabilities and promote adaptation. (p.306)

Service Coordination:

Often, a child with Autism and their family needs may range from linkage and referrals to guidance and assistance of a professional. Most referrals to for advocacy and support are made because an immediate need exists, or the family and/or child are in crisis and are in need of immediate advocacy and guidance. Parents should be taught about the numerous professional supports that are available to them (E.G. Homemaker, respite and childcare, transportation.) An assessment should be made of the autistic child's needs – immediate and long term- and a plan developed to work towards these and other valued outcomes. In addition, some of the venues of service provision can be very helpful and informative to the family of an autistic child:

- Outreach- Varied outreach activities such as, presentations at schools and community organizations; distribution of fliers to libraries, health fairs, religious organizations, MR/DD council committees and subcommittees.
- Advocacy- Advocating and Teaching parents and the individual self-advocacy skills through workshops and group forums
- Housing Resource Info- providing resource info for people with developmental disabilities and their families, who need assistance in obtaining accessible and affordable housing.
- Benefit advisement- assistance with navigating the system, which would include:
    o Filing for benefits
    o Appeals for denials
    o Overpayments.

Theory Behind The Solution:

As per Moxely and Jacobs, the concept of animation as a basic aspect of community organizing refers to the activation of people to take responsibility for their own affairs, with aim of achieving their own self-defined ends (p. 1). By integrating parents and sibling into a support network within the agency, they come together in spirit in trying to develop their own response to a community problem that is statistically growing: Autism. Through the parent's participation in the psycho-educational support groups, their independence, integrity, inclusion and productivity towards the issue of autism will enable to carry out what they have learned to the greater community. Animation, as per Moxley and Jacobs (1995) recognizes the importance of empowering others to resolve or respond to those problems that they see as critical by becoming a "means" or catalyst through which key stakeholders…can become a hallmark of organizations which incorporate animation as a principal program development strategy (p. 12). By gaining access to needed services and by providing the correct guidance in obtaining the right educational and transitional services for the autistic consumer, the service coordinator is also increasing the independence, integration, integrity, and productivity of the consumer to become a part of their community. It is the consumers' ability to function in the least restrictive environment that enables them to voice the "need" for more services for the autistic community through their own success.

As per Mayer (1985) The objective of the participatory model that is the advocacy of public or collective interests. The objective sought through this administrative model is the likelihood that plans will be implemented. Participatory models are designed to meet a third objective: to increase the fit between the interests reflected in the plan and those held by individuals on whose behalf plan making is undertaken (p. 93).

CHAPTER 6:

AUTISM AND THE FAMILY

Many autistic children and their families' are often in need of support and advocacy services throughout the child's lifespan. For one, research shows that mothers of autistic children show high levels of stress and reactive depression, and the marriage may suffer as well (Zeanah, 2000). The adaptation of parents, siblings, and other family members often varies over time, both as a result of the normative stress and transitions inherent in family life and as a result of the special needs of the autistic child. Research also indicates that parents of children with autism experience greater stress than parents of children with mental retardation and Down syndrome (Powers, 1989). This may be a result of the distinct characteristics that individuals with autism exhibit. An individual with autism may not be able to express their basic wants or needs. Therefore, parents are left playing a guessing game. A child's deficits in social skills, such as the lack of appropriate play, are also stressful for families. Individuals lacking appropriate leisure skills often require constant structure of their time, a task not feasible to accomplish in the home environment. Furthermore, many families struggle with the additional challenges of getting their child to sleep through the night or eat a wider variety of foods. All of these deficits and behaviors are physically exhausting for families and emotionally draining. Lastly, Parents of children with autism are grieving the loss of the "typical" child that they expected to have. In addition, parents are grieving the loss of lifestyle that they expected for themselves and family. The feelings of grief that parents experience can be a source of stress due its ongoing nature. When the needs of the family are being considered, more attention is being placed on the Autistic child and the "need" for the family to devote their time to managing the child's educational plan, while ignoring the need of the parent or caregiver. In this chapter I will explore the leading stress theorists in the field and how it applies to parenting an autistic child. I will also use examples from interviews and postings from a message board that I had founded and moderate on a daily basis. The names and some information were changed to protect the individual's identity, but the context of their situation was kept intact.

Lazarus (1966), a leading stress and coping theorist, suggested that psychological stress depends on cognitions relating to the person and the environment (Lazarus, 1990). He identified three basic types of stress: 1.) Systemic or Physiological – biological stress (i.e. increased blood pressure or heart rate, physical illness); 2.) Psychological – Cognitive evaluation of threat; and 3.) Social stress – Disruption of the social unit or system (domestic violence, substance abuse, and family conflict). According to Lazarus when a stressful event occurs, a person engages in a process of cognitive appraisal, evaluating of whether and in what ways an encounter is relevant to one's well-being. Cognitive appraisal consists of two phases. In the first phase, called primary appraisal, individuals evaluate an encounter's personal significance to their well-being. There are three types of primary appraisals - threat, challenge, and harm/loss, all of which are influenced by *goal relevance, ego involvement and goal congruency. Goal relevance* refers to the extent to which the encounter impacts valued personal goals; *Ego involvement* refers to the diverse aspects of ego identity or personal commitment that are at stake, and *Goal congruency* describes the degree to which the transaction facilitates or impairs goal attainment (Burton & Naylor, 1997). If a situation is appraised to cause a threat, challenge, harm or loss, the individual moves into Secondary appraisal, which is an evaluation of what, if anything can be done to overcome or prevent harm. Secondary appraisal focuses on assessing perceptions of how well the individual can handle or manage the encounter, that is, their coping resources (Burton & Naylor, 1997).

A common response to a stressor is coping. Coping refers to the thoughts and acts people use to manage the demands of stressful situations. Coping resources are the actual cognitive and behavioral techniques that individuals have at their disposal to deal with problems and improve emotional well-being. Lazarus and Folkman (1984) emphasize two major coping resources: Problem-focused coping and emotional focused coping. These thoughts and acts can be directed both at altering the troubled person-environment transaction (problem-focused coping) and regulating distressing emotions (emotion-focused coping). Coping is also seen as the constantly changing cognitive and behavioral efforts to manage specific external and/or internal demands that are appraised as taxing or exceeding the resources of the individual (Family) – (Lazarus and Folkman, 1984.). Coping varies as to the needs of the current stressful situation (e.g., Folkman & Lazarus, 1980; Matt, Wethington, & Kessler, 1990; Mechanic, 1978; Pearlin & Schooler, 1978) and as to the coping style and strategy of the individual (family) (Folkman & Lazarus, 1984; Thoitis, 1995). These resources are also influenced by coping styles, which are habitual preferences for approaching problems; these are more general coping behaviors that the individual employs when facing stressors across a variety of situations, as with raising a child diagnosed with autism (Thiotis, 1995).

Lazarus and Folkman (1984) emphasized the assessment of stress primarily from the viewpoint of an individual; stress, however, is perceived differently on a family level. Family Stress theorists focus on the roles that stress and coping play not only in individual but also family development. However, more is known about the stress that individuals experience in the family than is known about families under stress (Pearlin and Turner, 1987), which was the goal of some early stress research (Hill, 1949).

The importance of family stress theory in studying normative family transitions and adaptation to major life changes and illness is based on the central role that family strengths and capabilities play in understanding and explaining psychological and behavioral outcomes (Figley, 1989). In family stress theory, the family is "viewed as encountering hardships and changes as an inevitable part of family life over the life cycle" (McCubbin &McCubbin, 1993). Family stress theory provides a way of viewing the family's efforts over time to adapt to multiple stressors through using family resources and perceptual factors as a coping process aimed at achieving family balance (McCubbin & Patterson, 1981). A family situation addresses multiple changes and demands simultaneously, not single stressors. Secondary stressors, such as role change, responsibility, and caregiving demands, emerge from the primary stressors and these strains often may be difficult to resolve. They become instead a source of chronic strain. Chronic strain causes a build-up of unresolved stressors and contributes to undesirable characteristics in the family environment (Figley & McCubbin, 1983). A family system has a character of its own (Boss, 1988; Pemberton, 2005) separate than that of a single individual/member of the family. Parents are influenced by the stress experienced by other members of the family – including the autistic child (Kaplan, Smith, Grobstein, & Fischman, 1973; Thiotis, 1995).

One of the pioneer and widely used models for conceptualizing family stress is Hill's (1949) ABC- X model. Hill's model was formulated (1947, 1958) on the basis of extensive observations of families who survived the great depression and World War II. In his model the "A" stands for the activating event or stressor. The "B" stands for the resources or strengths that the person or family brings to the stressful situation. The "C" comprises the meanings that the family attaches to the event and the perception of their resources, and the "X" stands for crisis and stress.

Hill's (1949) ABCX Model of Stress and Coping

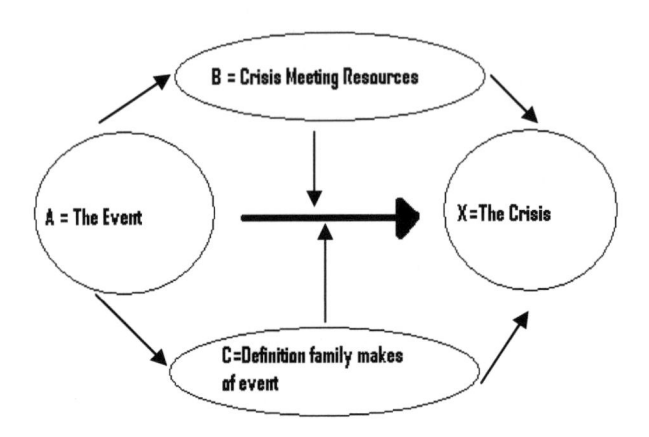

```
        B = Crisis Meeting Resources
           ↗              ↘
    ┌──────────┐     ┌──────────┐
    │ A = The  │ ──▶ │ X = The  │
    │  Event   │     │  Crisis  │
    └──────────┘     └──────────┘
           ↘              ↗
        C = Definition family makes
              of event
```

The degree of stress in Hill's theory is a continuous variable. Family crisis is brought about by such severe stress that the family cannot function and become immobilized. When crisis happens, the family goes on a roller-coaster profile of adjustment.

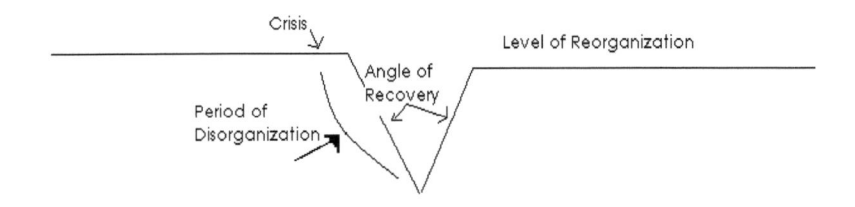

```
                Crisis                    Level of Reorganization
    ─────────────────↘───────────────────────────────────────
                      \      Angle of
            Period of  \    Recovery
         Disorganization↘   ↗
                          \/
```

The roller-coaster model includes the period of disorganization, the angle of recovery, and the level of reorganization after the crisis, indicating that post crisis adjustment may be below, equal to, or above the previous level of functioning (Hill, 1949). Use of this roller coaster model led to the concept of "stress pile-up," by McCubbin and Patterson (1983) who expanded on Hill's model with the development of the Double ABCX model of family adjustment.

The Double ABCX model expands the original ABC-X model by defining family stress as a state that arises from an imbalance between the demands and the family's resources for coping. Rather than looking at a single stressor event as in Hill's model, we look at a pile-up of demands (a,A,) that influence the current stressor that make adaptation more difficult. The same thing occurs with resources, existing and new (b,B) the meaning, or perception, the family assigns to the event (c,C) and the range of both positive and negative outcomes. The Double ABCX model may be useful in examining families of children diagnosed with autism for the following reasons: (a) addresses family stress in a chronically ill context (b) recognizes the social and contextual nature of adaptation over time (c) provides assessment of coping strategies and resources, and (d) addresses the possibility that healthy adaptation rather than pathology may characterize the family's response to stress (Glass, 2001). For example, Ms. T's Dependence on J's therapists for support was seen as a result of one of many perceived stressors that she had in caring for J.:

> ...Weekends are more stressful...basically I am with J. and E. ...I don't have the energy anymore lately, its kind of hard eating out...it is kind of difficult watching the both of them at the same time. One wants to go this way and another wants to go that way. We try to go out and go to the park but I know how he feels in certain places...If you have to walk him around the store forget it, he'll run and run...If there is a carriage its ok he's stable. Sometimes we try to do other indoors things. He went to three and four movies, but more of a private setting with the therapists who can manage his behaviors. We tried on his own, it was a dinosaur movie, and we thought he would like it but after 20 min he was stimming. The therapists will help with that. They would always help with that...

In the above quote, "A" would be the lack of supports that Ms. T. has, "B" would be T's adaptation to certain situations in her outings with her children, "C" would be the feelings of loss for the therapists who were a help to her and the "X" caregiver strain of caring for these children alone and attempting to adjust to that. Every time Ms. T would speak of the "Therapists" (Special Education Teachers) she always had a smile on her face, seeing them as a relief from the everyday stressors of mothering J.:

> ...They helped me get a lot of hours...once they sent the therapists...It was sort of connecting to another... I loved them so much...another therapist, more help, more ABA, speech...

> The therapists were good about referring from one to another so as to help my son. T. told me about B. and I got into her place, and as time went on...one referral to another...he was always in contact with these therapists that he played with them...everything was a help until august, when the age changed.

> *From the ages 18mths to four years everything was good...I am used to the competent people coming into my home helping me and J. ...in August that all stopped. I have nothing now...*

Further discussion into this area revealed methods of coping that Ms. T. now uses in relation to the care of her children "post-therapists":

> *...The three weeks in the summertime were the most difficult and I used to hope that the weeks would go by really fast...after not having this help I feel that I am "loosing it" more...*
>
> *...I Snap a J., and I find myself screaming at the kids more. I just put them in front of the TV because after a while you just need a break and I was not getting a break. The summer break was a tough ten days...I can't help J.... I would ask E. "why do you spend time with J." he would ask "why don't you play with me".*
>
> *...The only way to cope is to Just fight for you child...the more research you do the better you are...you need to keep up with the research, with the doctors...Sometimes I feel like I am going through the motions: get up, get the kids ready for school, doing my research, complaining to the school about one thing or another...I have gone to some support groups to learn from other's which made me feel better...*

The factors Ms. T identified as "stressful" parallel with Olsson and Hwang's (2002) research on the sense of coherence in parents of children with Autism. According to their study, parents of autistic children report higher stress and more adjustment problems that parents of Down syndrome children due to the behavioral problems of the autistic child. Ms. T identified numerous instances where J's behavior affected her coping with the situation, and blamed the behavior on the lack of supports that she now receives. "Everything was better" was a common phrase that was used throughout the interview when relating to J's therapists in comparison to the lack of services that she now perceives herself to receive.

There is little doubt that parenting a child with autism is extremely demanding. Because of the relatively poor understanding of autism by the general public when compared with other disabilities such as Down syndrome (Fisman, Wolf, & Noh, 1989), leading to a marked antipathy for the typical behavior exhibited by children with autism (Koegel et al., 1992), and also because of the socially inappropriate and aggressive nature of much autistic behavior, parents of children with autism often report high levels of anxiety, depression, and everyday stress from parenting (DeMeyer, 1979; Harris, 1984). This is further exacerbated when parents realize that there is no cure for autism and those services, which can be of real assistance, are often insufficient to meet parents' needs. In addition, as noted by Holroyd, Brown, Wikler, and Simmons (1975), the extra time which parents have to devote to their child with autism can sometimes make other children feel neglected, or cause conflict between siblings, thus exacerbating parental stress. Research data compiled by Rodrigue, Morgan, and Geffken (1990) also suggest that mothers of autistic children reported lower perceived parenting competence, which suggests that they may feel more uncertain about whether they possess the skills necessary to be a good parent relative to mothers of Downs Syndrome and developmentally normal children (Page 376). Parenting a child with autism has also been shown to have detrimental effects on marital relations (Piven, Chase, Landa, & Wzorek, 1991), since the thought basis of the "perfect family" system is thrown into chaos. A parent who posted on the message board that focuses on High functioning Autism (http://groups.yahoo.com/group/High_Functioning_Autism) outlines the effects of autism on her and her family:

> *I'm 46 and my son is 16. I've always tried to encourage my son in his interests and making sure he kept his focus. His struggles have taken a toll on his self esteem, and making and keeping friends has been hard. He's always fallen in with whoever would accept him, and these people are not friends you would approve of. He is learning his lesson on who he can trust and who he can't. Keep their self esteem nurtured because this will suffer as they get older and realize their differences. Encourage their creativity and their identity because these guys have brilliant viewpoints and abilities. Bombard them and stimulate them with everything you think they might be interested in. I know your children are young, but once they get in the school system. They will be forced to conform to the one size fits all culture of public school. Be diligent and militant if need be, to get them all the services they deserve. Many times I have felt alone, misunderstood, foggy and uncertain about my son. My marriage finally dissolved I believe, because of the struggle. Don't let this discourage you though. My husband wasn't willing to put the time and energy into my son's education like I did. Just make sure you're both putting your best efforts toward helping to build your children's lives. Just my two cents worth. God bless you and trust Him to help your family. You have 2 very beautiful flowers that spread and grow with every changing day......*

As per Zeanah (2002) it seems that supports, appraisals, and family coping strategies are important areas of strength that may mediate stress in families of children with disabilities and promote adaptation. (p.306). High information seeking is also seen as an adaptive coping response because it may impel parents to learn how to help their child effectively. Here is another example of a mother from the message board that seems to have educated herself on numerous therapies for her children, both diagnosed with autism:

> *I am 34 years old and I have 2 children with HFA. My son is 4 ½ and my daughter is 2 ½. My son's Autism was NOT caused by vaccines. Looking back he was Autistic from birth. There was a running joke that he was seeing ghosts because he would stare in the same place every day and NEVER look in your direction. When you would get close he would look away or close his eyes. He has made remarkable progress and he is a very talented mountain biker. Yes at 4 ½ he mountain bikes. Since he was 3 ½. The hard part was teaching him that he was not the only one on the trails!!! My daughter, A. was born with Acid reflux. I held her up-right for the first 4 months of her life. 24/7. We slept that way etc... If I put her down she would vomit. Luckily with previcid and some time she is over it. She was typically developing until 18 months. She rapidly went down hill. Stopped talking and stimming hard on everything. Some stims her brother never did. That is how I knew she was not copying him. She is in ABA and O.T and speech. She stopped banging her head and walking around with her eyes closed. But we have a long way to go. Me, I started making Weighted vests for mine and other children with sensory issues. I have donated to my son's class and made some for the local O.T. therapists. It is a personal joy of mine and it helps me be a stay at home mom. I am wishing to learn more about how I can help my angels grow wide, beautiful wings. It is very hard with my 2 but I know I am not alone even though I feel that way sometimes. With a*

> *little rain not only comes a rainbow but also flowers along the path. I often wonder what the future is for them it scares me to death. I try to take it one day at a time or I will just cry. One struggle at a time. And when I have the time to smell their freshly washed hair it is a great day! My little babies again.....*

High information seeking, however, also may suggest that mothers are relying solely on themselves to obtain information, rather than incorporating professional help into their support network. An example of this is shown with the following mother who also posted on the message board, who seems to be relying only on herself:

> *My youngest is 30 months old and was just diagnosed with Autism Spectrum Disorder. I am totally new to this and want to learn all about how I can do my best for her. She can say only 2 words but we taught her sign from a very early age so she can communicate that way. Our main problem is her hurting people as well as herself. She also screams. The screaming is terrible and I don't know how to help her. She has been diagnosed with Sensory Integration Disorder, ASD, Pyridoxine Dependency Seizure disorder, and GERD. I feel overwhelmed. I am trying to make my house very sensory so she can meet her needs, but it is so hard......*

Anxiety about one's competence in the parenting role may affect a parent's ability to implement services successfully. This seems particularly important for mothers of autistic children because treatment programs for autistic children usually require considerable parental involvement. (Rodrigue, Morgan & Geffkin, 1990, p. 376)

Research indicates that parents of children with autism experience greater stress than parents of children with mental retardation and Down syndrome (Powers, 1989). This may be a result of the distinct characteristics that individuals with autism exhibit. An individual with autism may not be able to express their basic wants or needs. Therefore, parents are left playing a guessing game. A child's deficits in social skills, such as the lack of appropriate play, are also stressful for families. Individuals lacking appropriate leisure skills often require constant structure of their time, a task not feasible to accomplish in the home environment. Furthermore, many families struggle with the additional challenges of getting their child to sleep through the night or eat a wider variety of foods. All of these deficits and behaviors are physically exhausting for families and emotionally draining. Lastly, Parents of children with autism are grieving the loss of the "typical" child that they expected to have. In addition, parents are grieving the loss of lifestyle that they expected for themselves and family. The feelings of grief that parents experience can be a source of stress due its ongoing nature. When the needs of the family are being considered, more attention is being placed on the Autistic child and the "need" for the family to devote their time to managing the child's educational plan, while ignoring the need of the parent or caregiver. Therefore, the measure of a child's behavior overall shows to have a positive correlation on the stress level felt by the family

This point of parental stress is further justified in a longitudinal study carried out by Baxter, Cummins, and Yiolitis (200), where stress attributed by parents to their family member with intellectual disability was investigated overall period of seven years in relation to specific foci of parental worry, and also in relation to stress attributed to the youngest sibling without a disability. The stress parents attributed to their family member with a disability were about double that attributed to the youngest sibling without a disability. However, multiple regression analysis revealed that the stress attributed to the sibling without a disability actually accounted for most of the variance in explaining the stress attributed to the family member with a disability. It is concluded that the stress attributed to any specific child may be an indicator of more general family stress. It was also found that, while the strength of parental worry decreased from time 1 to 2, the pattern of worries did not change over time, and nor did the specific foci of worry differentiate low-stressed from high-stressed parents. It is suggested that the latter result may be due to the inadequacy of the specific foci to cover all sources of parental stress over the duration of the study. (p. 105)

Perhaps to be expected, parents with a major illness or disability reported higher levels of anxiety, depression and daily stress than non-disabled or ill parents. While any task is more difficult when we are ill, the particularly demanding task of parenting a child with autism apparently is similarly exacerbated for those parents who are not well themselves, reinforcing the need for effective and frequent home help for those parents with a disability or illness. Furthermore, nearly two-thirds of the parents sampled had access to other family members for assistance in childcare. Although the differences were nonsignificant at traditional levels, there were consistently lower scores on depression, anxiety, daily level of stress and frequency of being stretched beyond their limits for those parents who did have access to family members for child care than for those parents with no such access. These parents also reported higher levels of confidence in handling their child's major difficulty (Sharpley, 1997, p. 25).

CHAPTER 7:

SUMMARY AND RECOMMENDATIONS

Utilizing the holistic perspective of the previous chapters in the examination of the biological, social and past and current policy provisions on autism, a number of problems in regards to educational movement and placement arose. Therefore, it may be feasible to recommend the following for future policy oriented considerations:

1.) **Education of Teachers**: Due to the nature of autism only recently becoming an educational classification, teachers and other educational professionals should be trained to understand the disorder and its severity. Personnel preparation, according to Munoz (1989), in the field of autism has been inadequate. Not only with teachers, but social workers, school psychologist, residential care, family counselors, and other professionals could benefit from intensive pre-service and in-service training on autism. However, state-programming policies may not be implemented fully unless the proposed interventions are perceived to meet local needs and convictions. (Munoz, p. 114) Community education is also needed to increase awareness of autism. Such efforts could generate support for the development and awareness of services in most communities.

These additional services can help families deal with the autistic child's behaviors without judgment and understanding.

2.) **Education of Medical Professionals**: According to Barnett (1995), early intervention with special needs child on a pre-school level can produce large short term benefits for children on their intelligence quotient (IQ), school achievement, grade retention, placement, and social adjustment. It is important that Pediatricians and other medical personnel receive the necessary training in recognizing the symptoms of autism, since they have frequent contact with the child and family. However, few university degree programs prepare professionals to work with autistic children and their families. Early intervention and treatment of autism can significantly decrease many maladaptive behaviors. Pharmacological management of an autistic child's behaviors can sometimes help decrease them to a more manageable level. A knowledge base of autism can help the pediatrician help the child and the family in a more effective way in this area.

3.) **Programmatic Changes**: Since the Department of education only funds 9% of the cost for Special education, the state and local government are left with paying the majority of the bill (91%). Recently the Department of Education – National Institute on Disability and Rehabilitation Research are advocating for programmatic changes that will focus on children with "severe problem behaviors." The institute feels that physical aggression, violence, and self-injurious behaviors are among the primary obstacles to full inclusion of children and youth with disabilities in age appropriate community-based activities and regular education settings (1997). The department has explored and agreed that these "children" respond best to a structured and non-aversive approach. The current methods, as shown in the *Digest of Education Statistics* (see Appendix), clearly shows the lack of movement of the autistic person to a less restrictive setting. Funding for training and implementation of a Lovaas or TEACCH style method can significantly increase the movement of autistic children to a least restrictive environment. It would also reduce the overall cost of special education due to decreased enrollment in a segregated setting. However, both programs have their drawbacks. For one, the Lovaas Style – intensive behavior modification program, the most statistically successful overall, can also be the most costly and demanding. The state and local Board of Education would have to initially invest more funds to provide a one-to-one student-teacher ratio to make the program most effective. Also, staff would have to provide the teaching and structure of the program to already overwhelmed families. The TEACCH program is less demanding, but there is less long-term research to show a specific movement into a least restrictive environment. Even though many autistic individuals have employment capabilities in adulthood, they still need the supervision of the TEACCH program to carry out these activities. Also, there is no evidence of the autistic individual moving off of an already overused SSI and welfare system. To be effective, an approach should be flexible in nature, rely on positive reinforcement, be re-evaluated on a regular basis and provide a smooth transition from home to school to community environments. A good program will also incorporate training and support systems for the caregivers as well. Rarely can a family, classroom teacher or other caregiver provide effective habilitation for a person with autism unless offered consultation or in-service training by a specialist knowledgeable about the disability. Lastly, students with autism should have training in vocational skills and community living skills at the earliest possible age. Learning to cross a street safely, to make a simple purchase or to ask assistance when needed are critical skills, and may be difficult, even for those with average intelligence levels. Tasks that enhance the person's independence, give more opportunity for personal choice or allow more freedom in the community are important.

4.) **Family Advocacy, Education and Support**: The benefits of involving parents in their children's education are well documented and routinely practiced by school social workers. Family involvement in the education of an autistic child at school and at home becomes more critical because the child's successful development of independent living skills and the family's ability to maintain the young person at home hinges partially on the comprehensiveness and continuity of the child's education (Munoz, 1989). Parents should be taught about the numerous professional supports that are available to them (E.G. Homemaker, respite and child care, transportation.) Parents should also be taught the importance of Behavior Modification and how to become more aware of what is on their child's Individual Education Plan (IEP). Parents must be allowed the option of focusing on their family needs without being blamed for their child's disability.

HCBS Policy Proposal:

In the following section I will outline a policy that I feel is needed in light of recent trends in the United States, and expansion, in essence, of the current Home and Community Based Services Program for the Developmentally disabled to include individuals who are High Functioning individuals with Autism and do not meet the criteria for coverage under OMRDD standards for care. The policy that I proposing would provide a medical/financial/integrative support subsidy to individuals with autism and or developmental disabilities that are higher functioning and that, due to behavioral concerns and issues, would need to be maintained in the community

Historical Background of HCBS:

Currently, OMRDD (New York State) and other states do not provide for those higher functioning adult Autistic individuals who's IQ score is within the normal range of functioning. These higher functioning individuals are usually categorized to receive services under the office of mental health, which historically does not have a wide support and advocacy system under OMRDD. According to Goldberg (2002) One reason that states were more inclined to pay for services to the developmentally disabled than to the mentally ill is that a well-organized lobby and voluntary services existed earlier for the former than for the latter. By the time families of the mentally ill came together in an advocacy organization (National Alliance for the Mentally Ill, or NAMI) in 1979, the times were less friendly to financing social services. (p. 60).

Problems that necessitate the policy:

Higher functioning Autistic individuals fall under the auspices of the office of mental health, for example, in New York State. The states, according to Goldberg (2002) though relieved by SSI, Disability Insurance (DI), Medicare, and Medicaid of 50 to 100 percent of the costs of maintaining the mentally ill in institutions, failed to replace these hospitals with outpatient services or community care. Many of the mentally ill elderly ended up in nursing homes where, unlike the situation with mental hospitals, Washington shared the costs with the states. Many younger mental patients landed on the streets. This turn of events, referred to as deinstitutionalization, "was not a policy mandated by statutory law" but "as unforeseen outgrowth of a series of federal entitlement programs having little to do with the severely mentally ill" (Grob, 1997, p. 55). Under the banner of this non-policy, many of the severely mentally ill were either reinstitutionalized or neglected.

Proposed Policy Description:

The policy that I propose is to provide a medical/financial/integrative support subsidy or wavier to individuals with autism and or developmental disabilities that are higher functioning and that, due to behavioral concerns and issues, would need to be maintained in the community. Currently, in order to receive HCBS services (in New York State for example), an individual would need to be eligible for Medicaid benefits and have an intelligence quotient under 69, which would place an individual within the mild range of mental retardation. The policy that I propose would address the following issues:

- Maximize opportunities for individual choice through person-centered planning; advance independence, inclusion and individual and family responsibility throughout the system.
- Create funding mechanisms that strengthen capacity to deliver individualized services;
- Preserve oversight systems to ensure the highest quality of services for all individuals.

- Assure that all providers promote the health, safety and protection of individuals through compliance with the highest standards of operation;
- Improve access to needed services and supports for eligible individuals; enhance flexibility within the services system;
- Promote user-friendly efficient and effective operations; and
- Encourage continued participation and open communication among all those involved in the system.

The individuals who qualify for this program would be individuals with a diagnosis of autism ads per the DSM-IV manual, be eligible for Medicaid or would be eligible for Medicaid under this wavier program. Since most high functioning adult individuals with autism would financially qualify based on an inability to work, this wavier program would enable individuals with autism to become eligible for most public assistance programs.

Since OMRDD in New York state has experience in dealing with the Home and Community Service Wavier programs for the Developmentally Disabled, the administrative auspices of this program will be lodged, including the roles of the private sector and of local, state would be overseen and monitored by OMRDD. The State Office of Mental Retardation would be monitored by the State's Commission of Quality of Care (CQC) who will monitor that the rights of these individuals are not being abused in any way.

Additional funding and monitoring could be delegated to the local and national chapter of the Autism Society of America.

The short and long term goals of the policy are as follows:

1. providing a quality of life comparable, to the extent practicable, to that of similarly situated families without a family member having or who is high functioning autistic;
2. maintaining family unity;
3. preventing premature or inappropriate out-of-home placement;
4. reuniting families;
5. enhancing parenting skills; and
6. Maximizing the potential of the family member with who is a high functioning autistic, which includes movement and integration into the job market, access to appropriate medical care and financial services.

One of the main objectives is to allow and encourage people with high functioning autism to take their rightful place in society. Access to all the facilities available to normal society is a prerequisite if such objectives are to become a reality. The barriers which prevent active involvement are largely a result of misunderstanding. On the one hand, the general public has a fear of all forms of disability and need to be reassured, through education and increased awareness, that people with autism will present no threat and can, through their participation, enhance their own enjoyment of any activity.

On the other hand parents, families and the people with autism themselves must accept the challenges which normal life presents. High Functioning People with autism should not be prevented from attempting activities through over protectiveness or timidity. Experience has shown that, given appropriate encouragement and instruction, people with autism can accomplish much which would, at first sight, appear beyond their competence. Embarrassment, awkwardness and confusion are less common in the person with autism than in the general public and onlookers. Such responses will only be eradicated through experience, explanation and familiarity.

The short and long term funding mechanism of this policy would be through Medicaid. As per Anderson, Lakin, Managan, & Prouty (1998) Liberal access to Medicaid Home and Community Based Services has documented clearly and consistently superior social and functional development in the community versus institutional living. (p.9). By allowing a wavier for high-Functioning individuals with Autism would help prevent the institutionalization of these individuals in state institutions and nursing facilities. The period of this policy would be indefinite, or would terminate once the High Functioning Individual with autism is fully integrated into society, and no longer requires the support services implemented by this program. The program would be carried out by non-profit organizations to keep the costs of maintaining this program low. According to Goldberg (2002) the united states already depends heavily on the private sector to deliver health and welfare services, usually with direct government financing in the case of Medicare and Medicaid or indirect support through the tax system for employer. Furthermore, the 1967 amendments to the Social Security Act authorized the state to purchase services from non-profit providers, and so did several other pieces of important legislation. Since there are many non-profit providers providing this service already, this method of privatization would be economically and financially feasible to incorporate this program through these existing agencies.

Policy Analysis:

The goals of the policy are just and democratic, for they allow individual freedoms of higher function individuals with autism not to be miss grouped with individuals who are schizophrenic, and not allow them to be neglected by the current mental health system which provides little to no supports for the mentally ill. The goals of this policy are legal, for they already mirror goals that are similar to the current OMRDD Home and Community Based Services program for individuals who are mentally retarded and developmentally disabled. The goals of the policy will contribute to the better quality of life for the Higher Functioning Autistic Individual by focusing on the independence, integration, and productivity of the individual. The person with high functioning autism will be encouraged to participate in all decision making processes which concern services provided for their benefit. The denial of such rights, according to Lakin, Managan, & Prouty (1998) is illogical and unnecessary and appropriate mechanisms must be found in the design and implementation of all such services. By allowing the individual to qualify for Medicaid benefits under a waiver due to their disability (for those who are still dependent on their parents) would allow the individual access to better health care, overall monitoring of their care and needs by a social service agency that provides service coordination, at home an supported employment and integration wherever needed, and the ability to live at home with appropriate care services, if needed. This mirrors a similar policy adopted in Sweden for the elderly to live in their own homes as long as possible. According to Ginsburg and Rosenthal (2002) this included generous funding of apartment renovation, transportation, shopping services, and day centers. The number of places in large custodial institutions declined. "Service Houses", where people live in their own apartments but can get services as needed, were developed. Rapid expansion of home help was crucial in allowing the elderly to live at home while freeing their family members for employment (p. 131). Since the majority of parents that care for autistic individuals are their mothers, this program would reduce the actual feminization of care for these individuals by providing access to supportive care in their homes.

Political Feasibility of Policy:

Since Autism is a growing epidemic, as stated earlier in this paper, there are a number of political action groups that would back up such a policy as this one. In the 1950s, as per Lakin, Managan, & Prouty (1998) advocacy influences first became evident in the United States when parents and persons with MR/DD, particularly as represented by the Association for Retarded Citizens (since renamed "the Arc"), began to advocate on behalf of families and individuals with mental retardation in state institutions. For one, a Congressional Autism Caucus sponsored by the National Alliance for Autism Research (NAAR), founded and co-chaired by U.S. Representative Chris Smith (R-NJ) and U.S. Representative Mike Doyle (D-PA), the Congressional Autism Caucus, also known as the Congressional Coalition for Autism Research & Education, currently includes 177 members from 43 states. In addition, the Congressional Autism Caucus formed on January 10, 2001 and is the first organization on Capitol Hill to call national attention to autism and the first Congressional Member Organization (CMO) to focus its efforts on autism spectrum disorders. The members of Congressional Autism Caucus are committed to improving research, education, and support services for people with autism spectrum disorders and support initiatives that are vital to the national effort to provide hope and answers to anxious parents of children with autism. The Congressional Autism Caucus aims to generate much needed interest in funding for autism research by holding briefings that will provide a bipartisan forum where autism issues and proposed solutions can be debated and discussed.

Historically, United States follows a Liberal Welfare regime. As per Esping-Anderson (1999) Liberal welfare regimes in their contemporary form reflect a political commitment to minimize the state, to individualize risks, and to promote market solutions. (p. 75). In the United States, the role of the family is Marginal – hence the family social policies and care initiative such as Nursing facilities, ECT; the market plays a central role in the U.S. economy while the state plays a marginal role in this area. The dominant mode of solidarity in the U.S. is on the individual, and the degree of decomodification is minimal. The United States follows somewhat more closely to Sen's idea of freedoms in a market economy. Sen (1999) argues that there is a need to combine the markets with the development of social opportunities as well as freedoms - substantive human freedoms. And, unlike Weiss he argues for a broad view of freedom, one that encompasses both processes and opportunities, and for recognition of "the heterogeneity of distinct components of freedom as the stronghold of the states capacity. This policy promotes these ideals by helping the integration of the High Functioning Autistic Individual into the workforce through supportive services, with the ultimate goal of the individual not to need these services on a long term basis.

Economic and Administrative Feasibility:

According to Kane, Kane, Ladd & Veazle (1998) The average Medicaid long-term care expenditure on persons sixty-five and older varies from $2, 720 in New York to $380 in Arizona. Likewise, payments fro Home and Community Based Services (HCBS) vary from $1,180 in New York State to $29 in Mississippi. Only a modest portion (28%) of the variance in total long-term care expenditures appears to be related to differences in population characteristics. For this policy to be implemented, the reallocation of revenues already incorporated from OMRDD's HCBS program would be used to support the program, which would present a cost savings. This approach in referred to in congress as pay-go funding (2003). The inherent danger of this approach is that thinning out fiscal resources among many programs may mean that the program may not be adequately funded. According to the Annual report from the New York State Commission on Quality of Care for the Mentally Disabled (1997-1998) in the last twenty years, New York's system of care has undergone dramatic changes with an increasing emphasis on developing community-based services to ensure the availability of a comprehensive service delivery system. The increasing availability of both community-based residential and non-residential services has significantly reduced the state's reliance on institutional settings to treat persons with mental disabilities. As part of the evolution of our state's system of care, voluntary agencies have come to play an increasing role in serving persons with disabilities. (p.23)

Currently, states such as New York State have no specific policy regarding services for High Functioning Autistic individuals, therefore making this policy a potential cost increase to Medicaid funding. However, the use of support systems indirectly would prevent multiple hospitalizations of these individuals due to the behaviors of these individuals and residential placement, therefore reducing costs in other areas. With one of the goals is to include these individuals into the workforce, it would mean a reduction in these individuals in receiving Social Security Income and the de-familization of care – therefore allowing caregivers of these individuals to re-enter the workforce.

Our understanding of autism has grown tremendously since it was first described in 1943. Some of the earlier searches for "cures" now seem unrealistic in terms of today's understanding of brain-based disorders. To cure means, "to restore to health, soundness, or normality." In the medical sense, there is no cure for the differences in the brain, which result in autism. However, we're finding better ways to understand the disorder and help people cope with the various symptoms of the disability. Some of these symptoms may lessen as the child ages; others may disappear altogether. With appropriate intervention, many of the autism behaviors can be positively changed, even to the point that the child or adult may appear to the untrained person to no longer have autism. The majority of children and adults will, however, continue to exhibit some symptoms of autism to some degree throughout their entire lives.

A generation ago, 90% of the people with autism were eventually placed in institutions. Today, as a result of appropriate and individualized services and programs, even the more severely disabled can be taught skills to allow them to develop to their fullest potential.

CHAPTER 8 :

AUTISM RESOURCES

Autism Network for Hearing and Visually Impaired Persons
7510 Ocean Front Avenue
Virginia Beach, Virginia, USA, 23451
(804) 428-9036
(800) 3-AUTISM
Fax: (804) 428-0019

Autism Research Institute (ARI)
4182 Adams Avenue
San Diego, California, USA 92116
(619) 281-7165
Fax: (619) 563-6840

Autism Society of America [ASA]
7910 Woodmont Avenue, Suite 650
Bethesda, Maryland, USA 20814-3015
(301) 657-0881
(800) 328-8476
Fax: (301) 657-0869
Website:http://www.autism-society.org/

Families for Early Autism Treatment (FEAT)
P.O. Box 255722
Sacramento, California, 95865-5722
(916) 843-1536

MAAP (More Advanced Autistic People) Services Inc.
P.O. Box 524
Crown Point, Indiana, USA, 46307
Phone/Fax: (219) 662-1311

National Alliance for Autism Research (NAAR)
414 Wall St., Research Park
Princeton, New Jersey 08540
(609) 430-9160
888-777-NAAR
Fax: (609) 430-9163
Email: naar@naar.org.
Website: http://babydoc.home.pipeline.com/naar/naar.htm

Web Based Resources:

Autism Information Center at CDC
Phone: 800.311.3435
Web: www.cdc.gov/ncbddd/autism/index.htm

Autism Society of America
Phone: 800.328.8476
Web: www.autism-society.org

Autism Treatment Network
Web: www.autismtreatmentnetwork.org

Center on Positive Behavioral Interventions and Supports (PBIS)
Web: www.pbis.org

Center for Implementing Technology in Education (CITEd)
Web: www.citededucation.org

Cure Autism Now
Phone: 888.828.8476
Web: www.cureautismnow.org

Family Center on Technology and Disability
Web: www.fctd.info/

Indiana Resource Center for Autism
Web: www.iidc.indiana.edu/irca

Interactive Autism Network
Web: www.ianproject.org/

MAAP Services for Autism & Asperger Syndrome
Web: www.asperger.org

National Alliance for Autism Research
Phone: 888.777.6227
Web: www.naar.org/

NIH Autism Research Network
Web: www.autismresearchnetwork.org/AN/

NIMAS Development and Technical
Assistance Centers

Web: http://nimas.cast.org

O.A.S.I.S. Online Asperger Syndrome
Information and Support
Web: www.aspergersyndrome.org/

Professional Development in Autism Center
Web: depts.washington.edu/pdacent/

Yale Developmental Disabilities Clinic
Web: www.autism.fm

ABA Providers:

California

Applied Behavior Consultants School (ABC)
4550 Harlin Drive
Sacramento, Ca 95826
Phone: 800-435-9888 or 916-568-1111
Fax: 916-568-1112
E-mail: jmorrow223@aol.com
Web site:
http://www.onlearn.com/abc.html

Austin Partnership
200 Marina Drive, Suite C
Seal Beach, CA 90740-6057
Phone: 562-431-9293]
Fax: 562-431-8386
E-mail: autismptnr@aol.com

Behavior Analysts, Inc/ S.T.A.R.S School (Strategic Teaching and Reinforcement System)
3329 Vincent Road
Pleasant Hill, CA 94523
Phone: 925-210-9378
Fax: 925-210-0436
E-mail: stars@corteks.com
Web site:
http://www.corteks.com/stars

Behavior Therapy and Family Counseling Clinic

32123 Lindero Canyon Road, Suite 302
West Lake Village, CA 91361
Phone: 818-706-9913, ext. 4
Fax: 818-706-6093
E-mail: btfcc@best.com
Web site: http://www.btfcc.com

Center for Autism and Related Disorders (CARD)
2061 Business Center Drive, Suite 202
Irvine, CA 92612
Phone: 949-833-7736
Fax: 949-833-7566

Center for Autism and Related Disorders (CARD)
5677 Oberlin Drive, Suite 200
San Diego, CA 92121
Phone: 619-558-4567
Fax: 619-558-9250

Center for Autism and Related Disorders (CARD)
23300 Ventura Boulevard
Woodland Hills, CA 91364
Phone: 818-223-0123
Fax: 818-223-0133
E-mail: cardla2@aol.com
Web site: http://www.cardhq.com

Center Valley Autism Project
1518 Coffee Road, Suite C
Modesto, CA 95355
Phone: 209-613-7220
Fax: 209-578-4272
Web site:
http://www.lovvas.com/cvapl.htm

Institute for Applied Behavior Analysis
5777 West Century Boulevard, Suite 675
Los Angeles, CA 90045
Phone: 310-649-0499
Fax: 310-649-3109
E-mail: iabala@attmail.com
Web site: http://www.iaba.com

Lovaas Institute for Early Intervention
2566 Overland Avenue, Suite 530
Los Angeles, CA 90064-3366

Phone: 310-840-5983 ext.100
Fax: 310-840-5987

UCLA Young Autism Project
Dept. of Psychology
1282A Franz Hall
Box 951563
Los Angeles, CA 90095
Phone: 310-825-2319
Fax: 310-206-6380
Valley Mountain Regional Center
P.O. Box 692290
Stockton, CA 95269
Phone: 209-473-0951
Fax: 209-473-0256

Connecticut

Innovative Developments for Educational Achievement (IDEA)
20 Washington Avenue, Suite 108
North Haven, CT 06473
Phone: 203-234-7401
Fax: 203-239-4348
E-mail: ideasb@cshore.com

Florida

Reaching Potentials, Inc.
7390 NW 5th Street, #9
Plantation, Fl 33317
Phone: 954-321-7393
Fax: 954-321-1019
E-mail: RpforAutism@hotmail.com or info@reachingpotentials.org
Web site:
http://www.reachingpotentials.org

Illinois

Illinois Early Autism Project
Linden Oaks Hospital
852 West Street
Naperville, IL 60540
Phone: 630-718-0313
Fax: 630-718-0314

Maryland

Community Services for Autistic Adults And Children (CSAAC)
751 Twinbrook Parkway
Rockville, MD 20851-1428
Phone: 301-762-1650
Fax: 301-762-5230
E-mail: csaac.org
Web site: http://csaac.org/index.html

Massachusetts

The May Institute
940 Main Street
P.O. Box 899
South Harwich, MA 02661
Phone: 508-432-5530
Fax: 508-432-3478
E-mail: information@mayinstitute.org
Web site: http://www.mayinstitute.org

The New England Center for Children
(NECC)
33 Turnpike Road
Southboro, MA 01772-2108
Phone: 508-481-1015
Fax: 508-485-3421
E-mail: ksenecal@necc.org
Web site: http://www.NECC.org

Michigan
The Association for Behavior Analysis
213 West Hall
Western Michigan University
1201 Oliver Street
Kalamazoo, MI 49008-5052
Phone: 616-687-8341 or 616-387-8342
Fax: 616-387-8354
E-mail: 76236.1312@compuserve.com
Web site: http://www.wmich.edu/aba/Autismwebfile.html

Minnesota

Families for Effective Autism Treatment of Minnesota
1821 University Avenue
Suite 324 South
St. Paul, MN 55104

Phone: 612-927-0017
E-mail: elarsson@worldnet.art.net
Web site: http://208.210.146.138/abta/

Nevada

Early Children Autism Program
Department of Psychology / 296
University of Nevada
Reno, NV 89557
Phone: 775-784-1128
Fax: 775-784-1126

New Jersey

Alpine Learning Group
777 Paramus Road
Paramus, NJ 07652
Phone: 201-612-7800
Fax: 201-612-7710

Bancroft School
P.O. Box 20
Hopkins Lane
Haddonfield, NJ 08033-0018
Phone: 800-774-5516 or 856-429-0010
Fax: 856-429-4755
E-mail: Inquiry@Bancroftneurohealth.org
Web site: http://www.Bancroftneurohealth.org

Douglas Developmental Disabilities Center
Rutgers, the State University of New Jersey
25 Gibbons Circle
New Brunswick, NJ 08901-8528
Phone: 732-932-9137
Fax: 732-932-8081
Web site: http://www.rci.rutgers.edu/~gsapp/gsappweb/dddc.html

Douglas Outreach
Rutgers, the State University of New Jersey
30 Gibbons Circle
New Brunswick, NJ 08901-8528
Phone: 732-932-3902 Fax: 732-932-4469
E-mail: kdvorak@rutgers.edu

Eden Family of Services
One Logan Drive
Princeton, NJ 08540
Phone: 609-987-0099
Fax: 609-987-0243
E-mail: EdenSvcs@aol.com
Web site: http://members.aol.com/EdenSvcs/index.html

New Jersey Institute for Early Intervention
52 Haddonfield-Berlin Road,
Suite 4000
Cherry Hill, NJ 08034-3502
Phone: 856-616-9442
Fax: 856-616-9454

Partners in Therapy, Inc.
804 Park Avenue
Collingswood, NJ 08034-3502
Phone: 856-858-3673
Fax: 856--869-9469
E-mail: partner1@ix.netcom.com

Princeton Child Development Institute
300 Cold Soil Road
Princeton, NJ 08540-2002
Phone: 609-924-6280
E-mail: njpcdi@earthlink.net
Web site http://www.pcdi.org

Rutgers Autism Program
41 Gordon Road, Suite A
Piscataway, NJ 08854
Phone: 732-445-1141
Fax: 732-445-7970
Web Site: http://www.rci.rutgers.edu/~rapsite

New York

Center for Autism and Related Disorders (CARD)
280 North Central Avenue, Suite 314
Hartsdale, NY 10530
Phone: 914-683-3833
Fax: 914-683-3836

Eden II Programs / Genesis School

150 Granite Avenue
Staten Island, NY 10303
Phone: 718-816-1422
E-mail: eden2si@aol.com
Web site: http://www.eden2.org

Fred S. Keller School
1 Odell Plaza
South Westchester Executive Park
Yonkers, NY 10701
Phone: 914-956-1152
Fax: 914-956-1419

New York State Department of Educaton

Lawrence Gloeckler, Deputy Commissioner
Office of Vocational & Educational Services
for Individuals with Disabilities
1 Commerce Plaza, Room 1606
Albany, NY 12234
(518) 474-2714

**Programs For Children With Disabilities:
Ages 3 Through 5**

Michael Plotzker, Director
State Education Department
Special Education Services
1 Commerce Plaza, Room 1607
Albany, NY 12234
(518) 473-6108

**Programs For Infants And Toddlers With Disabilities:
Ages Birth Through 2**

Donna Noyes, Director
Early Intervention Program
Bureau of Child and Adolescent Health
Corning Tower, Room 208
Albany, NY 12237
(518) 473-7016
E-mail: dmn02@health.state.ny.us

State Vocational Rehabilitation Agency

Lawrence Gloeckler, Deputy Comm.
Office of Vocational and Educational Services
for Individuals with Disabilities
Department of Education
1 Commerce Plaza, Room 1606
Albany, NY 12234
(518) 474-2714

State Mental Health Agency

James Stone, Commissioner
Office of Mental Health
44 Holland Avenue
Albany, NY 12229
(518) 474-4403

State Mental Health Representative For Children And Youth

Michael Zuber
Office of Children & Families
Office of Mental Health
44 Holland Avenue
Albany, NY 12229
(518) 473-6902

OMRDD

Thomas Maul, Commissioner
NY State Office of MR and DD
44 Holland Avenue
Albany, NY 12229
(518) 473-1997

State Developmental Disabilities Planning Council

Sheila Cary, Director
NYS DD Planning Council
155 Washington Avenue, 2nd Floor
Albany, NY 12210
(518) 432-8233

Protection And Advocacy Agency

Marcel Chaine, Director Advocacy Bureau
NY Comm. on Quality of Care
99 Washington Avenue, Suite 1002
Albany, NY 12210
(518) 473-7378

CLIENT ASSISTANCE PROGRAM

Michael Peluso, CAP Director
NY Comm. on Quality of Care
99 Washington Avenue, Suite 1002
Albany, NY 12210
(518) 473-7378

Programs For Children With Special Health Care Needs

Christopher A. Kus, Director
Bureau of Child and Adolescent Health, Dept. of Health
Tower Building, Room 208
Albany, NY 12237-0618
(518) 474-2084
E-mail: cak03@health.state.ny.us

State Agency For The Visually Impaired

Thomas Robertson, Assistant Commissioner
Comm. for the Blind and Visually Handicapped
Department of Social Services
40 North Pearl Street
Albany, NY 12243
(518) 473-1801

Programs For Children And Youth Who Are Deaf Or Hard Of Hearing

Sharon Brown-Levey, Resource on Deafness
Office of Vocational and Educational Services
for Individuals with Disabilities
State Education Department
One Commerce Plaza, Room 1603
Albany, NY 12234
(518) 474-5652 (V/TTY)
(800) 222-5627 (V/TTY)

State Education Agency Rural Representative
Suzanne Spear, Supervisor
Department of Education
Bureau of School District Reorganization Unit
Education Building Annex, Room 876
Albany, NY 12234
(518) 474-3936

Christine McMahon, Chief Operating Officer
New York Easter Seal Society
845 Central Avenue
Albany, NY 12206
(518) 438-8785

Michael Reif, Director
Regional Early Childhood Direction Center
(Serving children birth to 5 and their families)
Box 671
601 Elmwood Avenue
Rochester, NY 14642
(800) 462-4344; (716) 275-2263
(Call to find out the Early Childhood Direction Center serving your community.)

Richard Warrender, State Advocate
State Advocate for Persons with Disabilities
1 Empire State Plaza, Suite 1001
Albany, NY 12223-1150
(518) 474-2825 (V); (518) 473-4231 (TTY)
(800) 522-4369 (V/TTY/Spanish, in NY only)
URL: http://www.state.ny.us/disabledadvocate

University Affiliated Programs
Madeline W. Appell, Director
DD Center/St. Lukes - Roosevelt Hospital Center
1000 10th Avenue
New York, NY 10019
(212) 523-6230

Ansley Bacon, Director
WIHD/University Affiliated Program

Westchester County Medical Center
Valhalla, NY 10595
(914) 285-8204
E-mail: Ansley_Bacon@NYMC.edu

John A. Kessler, Director
Univ. Affiliated Program/Rose F. Kennedy Center
Albert Einstein Coll. of Medicine/Yeshiva University
1410 Pelham Parkway South
Bronx, NY 10461
(718) 430-4228

Philip W. Davidson, Director
Strong Center for Developmental Disorders
University of Rochester Medical Center
601 Elmwood Avenue, Box 671
Rochester, NY 14642
(716) 275-2986

Technology-Related Assistance

Deborah Buck, Project Director
New York State TRAID Project
Office of Advocate for Persons with Disabilities
One Empire State Plaza, Suite 1001
Albany, NY 12223-1150
(518) 474-2825 (V); (800) 522-4369 (V/TTY/Spanish, in NY)
(518) 473-4231 (TTY)
URL: http://www.state.ny.us/disabledadvocate

Parent Training & Information Project

Joan M. Watkins, Executive Director
Parent Network Center
250 Delaware Avenue, Suite #3
Buffalo, NY 14202
(716) 853-1570; (800) 724-7408 (In NY)
(716) 853-1573 (TTY)

Galen Kirkland
Advocates for Children of New York (NY City)
105 Court Street, 4th Floor
Brooklyn, NY 11201
(718) 624-8450
E-mail: advocat1@idt.com

Karen Schlesinger, Director
200 Park Avenue South, Suite 816
New York, NY 10003
(212) 667-4650
E-mail: resourcesnyc@prodigy.net

Richard Lash, Executive Director
Singergia/Metropolitan Parent Center
15 West 65th Street, 6th Floor
New York, NY 10023
(212) 496-1300
E-mail: Sinergia@panix.com
URL: http://www.panix.com/~sinergia

Parent-To-Parent

Linda Rippel, Director
Parent to Parent of New York State
500 Balltown Road
Schenectady, NY 12304
(800) 305-8817; (518) 381-4350
E-mail: Parent2Par@aol.com
URL: http://www.parenttoparentnys.org

Mary Bonsignore, Project Coordinator
Family Support Project for the DD
North Central Bronx Hospital
3424 Kossuth Avenue, Room 15A10
Bronx, NY 10467
(718) 519-4797

Parent Teacher Association (Pta)

Carolyn Fiori, President
New York State Congress of Parents and Teachers, Inc.
One Wembley Square
Albany, NY 12205-3830
(518) 452-8808

<u>North Carolina</u>

Building Blocks Children's Group
1102 North Main Street, Suite 202
High Point, NC 27262
Phone: 336-886-8019

Fax: 336-886-8661
E-mail; BBlkChldGr@aol.com

Center for Autism and Related disorders
(CARD)
3711 W. Market Street, Suite B
Greensboro, NC 27403
Phone: 336-855-1700
Fax: 336-855-1787

Meredith Autism Program
Meredith College- Department of
Psychology
3800 Hillsborough Street
Raleigh, NC 27607-5298
Phone: 919-760-8080 Fax: 919-760-2303

Oregon

Project PACE, Inc.
9725 SW Beaverton Hillsdale Highway
Suite 230
Beaverton, OR 97005
Phone: 503-643-7015 Fax: 503-641-3640
E-mail: hred@projectpace.com
Web site: http://www.projectpace.com

Pennsylvania

The Childhood Learning Center
98 Fairview Street
Reading, PA 19605
Phone: 610-929-9459
Fax: 610-929-4066
E-mail: cynthia@tclc.com or info@tclc.com
Web site: http://www.tclc.com

Pittsburgh Young Autism Project
Intercare - Brentwood Office
4411 Stilley Road / Route 51
2nd floor, Suite 202
Pittsburgh, PA 15227
Phone: 412-881-3902
Fax: 412-881-3599

South Carolina

Autism Research Center, S.C.
P.O Box 1066
Anderson, SC 29622
Phone: 864-260-9005
Fax: 864-226-8902
E-mail: drbmetzger@aol.com

Texas

Texas Young Autism Project
Department of Psychology
University of Houston
Houston, TX 77204-5341
Phone: 713-743-8610
Web site: http://www.uh.edu/tyap

Terri Locke
Behavior Consultant, Parent Training,
Home & School Intervention,
Vocational & Functional Life Skills Training
Phone (published with permission)
210-771-3166

Busy Bodies
Sue Selander
San Antonio, TX
Gross Motor Movements & skills with ABA approach,
Handwriting & School Help
210-545-2840

Virginia

Center for Autism and Related Disorders (CARD)
5105-P Backlick Road
Annandale, VA 22003
Phone: 730-256-6383
Fax: 703-256-6384

Washington

Northwest Young Autism Project
Department of Psychology

Washington State University
P.O Box 644820
Pullman, WA 99164
Phone: 509-335-7750
Fax: 509-335-2522

Wisconsin

Autism and Behavioral Consultants
349 Winnebago Drive
Fond du Lac, WI 54935
Phone: 920-926-1255
Fax: 920-921-1798

Families with Autism Counseling and Resource Center
49 Kessle Court
Madison, WI 53711
Phone: 608-231-300, ext. 350

Integrated Developmental Services
14 Ellis Potter Court
Madison, WI 53711
Phone: 608-441-0123
Fax: 608-441-0126

Wisconsin Early Autism Project (W.E.A.P)
272 East Walnut Street
Green Bay, WI 53711
Phone: 920-431-3380
Fax: 920-431-0256
E-mail: weapgd.jobs.@wiautism.com

Wisconsin Early Autism Project (W.E.A.P.)
2433 North Mayfair Road, Suite 102
Wauwatosa, WI 53226
Phone: 414-479-9798
Fax: 414-479-9805
E-mail: weapmil.jobs@wiautism.com

Help With Training Or Programs:

The Young Autism Project at UCLA
UCLA Dept. of Psychology
405 Hilgard Avenue
Los Angeles, California 90024-1563

310-825-2319 tel.
310-206-6173 fax

The Early Childhood Intervention Center, Inc.
2124 Broadway, #338
New York, NY 10023
212-606-2036, Fax 212-877-1276.

Rutgers Center for Applied Psychology
41 Gordon Rd.
P.O. Box 5062
New Brunswick, N.J. 08903-5062
phone: 732-445-7778
extension #18: Ellen Picollo

Ivar O. Lovaas
1-310-825-2319
lovaas@psych.sscnet.ucla.edu
Note - Ivar Lovaas usually doesn't answer mail sent to this ID.

Center for Autism and Related Disorders, CARD.
CARD is run by Dr. Doreen Granpeesheh who did her PhD under Dr.Lovaas.
CARD does in-home workshops around the world.
CARD will come to your house within 3 weeks of contact.
Phone = 818-995-4673
Fax = 818-995-4679

Behavioral Intervention Associates (B.I.A.)
14 Crow Canyon Court, Suite 100
San Ramon, CA 94583
Tel: (510) 855-1350
The director of the program is Hilary Stubblefield

Wisconsin Early Autism Project
Child & Family Psychological Services
2828 Marshall Court, Suite110
Madison, Wi 53705
(608) 233-1551 Sally Brockett, M.S., Director

Innovative Developments for Educational Achievement, Inc. (IDEA)
20 Washington Ave., Suite 108
North Haven, CT 06473
203-234-7401

The May Center for Early Childhood Education
10 Acton Street
Arlington, MA 02174 Phone: (617)648-9260

NECA
33 Turnpike Road
Southboro, MA
(508)481-1015

Autism Partnership
Directors: Dr. Ronald Leaf & Dr. John McEachin
3346 Olive Avenue
Signal Hill, CA 90807
(310) 424-9293

Valley Mountain Regional Center
P.O. Box 692290
Stockton, California 95269-2290
209-473-0951 tel.

Alta California Regional Center
2031 Howe Avenue, Suite 100
Sacramento, California 95825
916-929-0500 tel.
Glen Sallows, Ph.D.

Wisconsin Early Autism Project
2828 Marshal Court, Suite 110
Madison, Wisconsin 53705
608-233-1551
608-836-9131

Eric Hamlin
Project PACE
Beaverton, Oregon
(503) 643-7015
(503) 641-3640 fax

Dr. Patty Matesky
Allegheny General Hospital
412-359-3160

Dr. Carryl Navalta
Lovaas Study
May Institute

10 Acton Street
Arlington, MA 02174
617-648-9260

Tristram Smith, Ph.D.
Washington State University
Pullman, Washington 99164-4820
509-335-7750

Dr. John McEachin
Autism Partnership
3346 Olive Avenue
Signal Hill CA 90807
(310) 424-9293, ext. 306 for Dr. McEachin, ext. 375 for Dr. Leaf

Greg Bunch, Ph.D.
3116D Oak road, Suite 106
Walnut Creek, California 94596
(510)938-4508

Doreen GranPeesheh, PhD.
Center for Autism and Related Disorders (CARD)
15840 Ventura Boulevard, Suite 301
Encino, California 91436
818-995-4679 tel.

Keli Larson, M.A.
1508 8th Avenue, Northeast
Rochester, Minnesota 55906
(507)282-0516

The Center for Applied Psychology - Rutgers University
New Brunswick, New Jersey
908-445-7778 tel.

ABC, Applied Behavior Consultants
Dr. Morro
Phone = 1-800-435-9888

Partners In Therapy, Inc.
804 Park Avenue
Collingswood, N.J. 08108
609-858-3673

Sandra J. Rowan, M.A.
Comunidad Los Horcones
Apartado Postal #372
Hermosillo Sonora Mexico
CP 83000
Tel/Fax (62) 14 72 19
E-Mail: walden@imparcial.com.mx

Ethel W. Hetrick, Ph.D. (Director)
Oak Forest Psychological Services
2834 Bill Owens Pkwy.
Longview, Texas 75605
Office: (903) 759-6588
Fax: (903) 759-4904
EHetrick1@aol.com

BOOKS:

- Baldi, H., & Detmers, D. (2000). *Embracing play: Teaching your child with autism* [Video]. Bethesda, MD: Woodbine House. (Phone: 800.843.7323; Web: www.woodbinehouse.com)

- Beytien, A. (2004). *Family to family: A guide to living life when a child is diagnosed with an autism spectrum disorder* [Video]. Higganum, CT: Starfish Specialty Press. (Phone: 877.782.7347; Web: www.starfishpress.com)

- Bondy, A., & Frost, L. (2002). *A picture's worth: PECS and other visual communication strategies in autism*. Bethesda, MD: Woodbine House.

- Bruey, C.T. (2003). *Demystifying autism spectrum disorders: A guide to diagnosis for parents and professionals*. Bethesda, MD: Woodbine House.

- Cafiero, J.M. (2005). *Meaningful exchanges for people with autism: An introduction to augmentative & alternative communication*. Bethesda, MD: Woodbine House.

- DuCharme, R., & Gullotta, T.P. (Eds.) (2004). *Asperger syndrome: A guide for professionals and families.* New York: Springer Publishers. (Phone: 800.777.4643; Web: www.springeronline.com)

- Glasberg, B. (2005). *Functional behavior assessment for people with autism: Making sense of seemingly senseless behavior.* Bethesda, MD: Woodbine House.

- *Journal of Autism and Developmental Disorders.* New York: Springer Publishers.

- Mesibov, G.B., Shea, V., & Schopler, E. (2004). *The TEACCH approach to autism spectrum disorders.* New York: Springer Publishers.

- O'Brien, M., & Daggett, J.A. (2006). *Beyond the autism diagnosis: A professional's guide to helping families.* Baltimore, MD: Brookes Publishing (Phone: 800.638.3775; Web: www.brookespublishing.com)

- Richman, S. (2000). *Raising a child with autism: A guide to applied behavior analysis for parents.* London: Jessica Kingsley Publishers. (Web: www.jkp.com/)

- Tsai, L.Y. (1998). *Pervasive developmental disorders.* Washington, DC: NICHCY. (Available online at: www.nichcy.org/pubs/factshe/fs20txt.htm)

- Volkmar, F.R., & Wiesner, L.A. (2003) *Healthcare for children on the autism spectrum: A guide to medical, nutritional, and behavioral issues.* Bethesda, MD: Woodbine House.

- Wiseman, N.D. (2006). *Could it be autism?* New York: Broadway Books. (Web: www.broadwaybooks.com)

First Books

- Powers, M. (1999). *Children with autism: A parent's guide.* Second edition. Rockville, MD: Woodbine House.
- Satkiewicz-Gayhardt, V. Peerenboom, B. & Campbell, R. (1997). *Crossing Bridges: A parent's perspective on coping after a child is diagnosed with autism/PDD.*

Autism Overview

- Grandin, T. (1995). *Thinking in pictures and other reports from my life with autism.* New York: Doubleday. [first person account]
- Gerlach, E.K. (1999). *Just this side of normal: Glimpse into life with autism.* [parent perspective]

- Peeters, T. (1997). *Autism: From theoretical understanding to educational intervention*. London: Whurr Publishers

Asperger Syndrome: Overview

- Attwood, T. (1998). *Asperger's syndrome: A guide for parents and professionals*. London: Jessica Kingsley Publications.
- Fling, E (2000). *Eating an Articoke: A mother's perspective on asperger syndrome*.
- Willey, L.H. (2001). *Asperger syndrome in the family*. Philadelphia, PA: Jessica Kingsley Publishers [first person account]

Support for Families

- Harris, S. (1994). *Siblings of children with autism: A guide for families*. Rockville, MD: Woodbine House.
- Maurice, C. (1993). *Let me hear your voice*. New York: Fawcett Columbine.
- Meyer, D. & Vadasy, P. (1994). *Sibshops: Workshops for siblings of children with special needs*. Baltimore, MD: Brookes Publishing.
- Schopler, E. (1995). *Parent survival manual: A guide to crisis resolution in autism and related developmental disorders*. New York: Plenum [for parents of children ages 8 and older]

Books written for siblings and peers about Autism

- *Russell is Extra Special* by Charles Amenta [autism]
- *Someone Special, Just Like You* by Tricia Brown [disabilities]
- *Ian's Walk* by Laurie Lears [autism]
- *Talking to Angels* by Esther Watson [autism]

First Steps to Treatment:

- Bondy, A. (2001). *A picture's worth: PECS and other visual communication strategies in autism*. Bethesda, MD: Woodbine House.
- Gutstein, S. & Sheely, R. (2002). *Relationship development intervention with young children*. London: Jessica Kingsley.
- Hodgdon, Linda (1996) *Visual strategies for improving communication*. Troy, MI: QuirkRoberts Publishing.
- Kranowitz, C. (2003). *The out-of-sync child has fun*. New York: Perigee.
- Maurice, C. (1993). *Let me hear your voice*. New York: Fawcett Columbine.

- Maurice, C., Green, G. & Luce, S. (1996). *Behavioral intervention for young children with autism.* Austin, TX: Pro-Ed.
- Quill, K. (2000). *DO-WATCH-LISTEN-SAY: Social and communication intervention for children with autism.* Baltimore, MD: Brookes Publishing.
- Sonders, S. (2002). *Giggle time - Establishing the social connection: A program to develop the communication skills of children with autism.* London: Jessica Kingsley.
- Sussman, F. (1999). *More than words: Helping parents promote communication and social skills in children with autism spectrum disorder.* Toronto, Canada: Hanen Centre Publication.
- Weiss, M.J. & Harris, and S.L. (2003) *Right from the start: Behavioral intervention for young children with autism: A guide for parents and professionals.* Bethesda, MD: Woodbine House.
- Wolfberg, P. (2003). *Peer play and the Autism spectrum.* Shawnee Mission, KS: AAPC.

Autism: Intervention guidelines

- Beyer, J. & Gammeltoft, L. (2000). *Autism and play.* London: Jessica Kingsley Publications.
- Greenspan, S. & Weider, S. (1998). *The child with special needs: Encouraging intellectual and emotional growth.* New York: Addison-Wesley.
- Janzen, J. (1996). *Understanding the nature of autism: A practical guide.* SanAntonio, TX: Therapy Skill Builders.
- Partington, J. & Sundberg, M. (1998). *The assessment of basic language and learning skills (ABLLS): An assessment and curriculum guide for children with autism and other language delays.* Danville, CA: Behavior Analysts, Inc.
- Quill, K. (1995). (Ed.) *Teaching children with autism: Strategies to enhance communication and socialization.* Albany, NY: Delmar.
- Sussman, F. (1999). *More than words: Helping parents promote communication and social skills in children with autism spectrum disorder.* Toronto, Canada: Hanen Centre Publication.

Asperger's Syndrome: Intervention guidelines

- Gagnon, E. (2002). *Power Cards: Using special interests to motivate children and youth with Asperger syndrome and autism.* Shawnee Mission, KS: AAPC.
- Gray, C. (2000). *The new Social Story book.* Arlington, TX: Future Horizons.
- Gutstein, S.E. & Sheely, R.K. (2002) *Relationship development intervention with children, adolescents and adults: Social and*

- *emotional development activities for Asperger Syndrome, Autism, PDD and NLD*. Philadelphia, PA: Jessica Kingsley Publishers.
- Moyes, R.A. (2002). *Addressing the challenging behavior of children with high functioning autism and Asperger syndrome in the classroom*. Philadelphia, PA: Jessica Kingsley.
- Myles, B.S. & Adreon, D. (2001). *Asperger syndrome and adolescence: Practical solutions for school success*. Shawnee Mission, KS: AAPC.
- Myles, B. S. & Southwick, J. (1999). *Asperger syndrome and difficult moments: Practical solutions for tantrums, rage and meltdowns*. Shawnee Mission, KS: AAPC.
- Quill, K. (1995). (Ed.) *Teaching children with autism: Strategies to enhance communication and socialization*. Albany, NY: Delmar.

Inclusion:

- Doyle, M. (1997). *The paraprofessional's guide to the inclusive classroom*. Baltimore, MD: Paul H. Brookes.
- Giangreco, M. (1997). *Quick - Guides to Inclusion: Ideas for educating students with disabilities*. Baltimore, MD: Paul H. Brookes.
- Giangreco, M. (1997). *Quick - Guides to Inclusion 2: Ideas for educating students with disabilities*. Baltimore, MD: Paul H. Brookes.
- Wagner, S. (2001). *Inclusive programming for elementary school students with autism*. Arlington, TX: Future Horizons.
- Wagner, S. (2001). *Inclusive programming for middle school students with autism*. . Arlington, TX: Future Horizons.

CATALOGS

Resource catalogs specializing in Autism and Asperger syndromes:

- Autism Asperger Publishing Co 1-913-897-2632 www.asperger.net
- Autism Society of North Carolina 1-919-743-0204 www.autismsociety-nc.org
- Autism Resource Network 1-952-988-0088 www.autismbooks.com
- Different Roads to Learning 1-800-853-1057 www.difflearn.com
- Future Horizons 1-800-489-0727 www.futurehorizons-autism.com
- Jessica Kingsley Publishers 1-800-634-7064 www.jkp.com

Resource catalogs for instructional materials:

- Scholastic Book Club 1-800-724-2424
- Lakeshore Learning Materials 1-800-421-5354
- PCI Educational Publishing 1-800-594-4263

- LinguiSystems 1-800-776-4332
- Mayer-Johnson Co. 1-619-550-0084
- Edmark 1-800-362-2890
- Academic Communication Assoc. 1-619-758-9593
- Don Johnston 1-800-999-4660
- Imaginart Communication Products 1-800-828-1376
- SuperDuper School Company 1-800-277-8737
- ABC School Supply 1-800-669-4222
- PRO-ED 1-800-897-3202

VIDEOS

First Video:

- Attainment Company (1998). *Straight talk about autism with parents and kids: Childhood issues.* (parents of newly diagnosed children). To order, call 1-800-327-4269.

Early Intervention Videos:

- Minnesota Autism Network (1999). *Promising Practices: Effective early intervention in autism* (excellent video for professionals and families serving children, ages birth-to-5). To order, call Metro ECSU at 1-612-706-0801.
- Greenspan, S. & Wieder, S. (2000). *Floor Time strategies.* Training videotapes. To order, call the Interdisciplinary Council on Developmental and Learning Disorders, Bethesda, MD at 1-301-656-2667.
- Murphy, K. & Rouse, C. (1997). *How to set up your home to help the nonverbal child.* (practical use of AAC for nonspeaking children). To order, contact Mayer Johnson at 1-619-550-0084.
- New York Families for Autistic Children (1999). *Family Educational Series: Discrete Trial Teaching, Play Skills, and Behavior Management.* (video series). To order, call 1-718-641-6711.

Autism: Videos

- Goodman, J. & Hoban, S. (1992). *Day by Day: Raising children with autism/PDD.* New York, NY: Guilford Publications.
- Grandin, T. (1999). *The autism continuum: Perspectives on autism from first-person account.* Available through Future Horizons Publishing Company.
- Indiana Resource Center (1997). *Sense of belonging: Including students with autism in their school community.* (practical suggestions

using elementary and middle school case studies). To order, call the Indiana Resource Center at 1-812-855-6508.
- University of Washington (1995). *Samantha: A story about positive behavior support.* (illustrates steps in the assessment and treatment of challenging behaviors). To order, call the Center on Human Development and Disability at 1-206-543-4011.

Instructional Videos developed as learning tools for children with autism

- Special Kids: Video programs that teach self-care, social, language and academic skills. To order, call 1-800-KIDS-153 or www.specialkids.com
- Joining in: A program for teaching social skills by Murdock. To order, contact Autism Asperger Publishing company www.asperger.com

For more information, books, and videos on autism spectrum disorders, the *Autism Society of North Carolina Bookstore* has over 400 titles in their collection. (Phone: 919.743.0204; Web: www.autismbookstore.com)

BIBLIOGRAPHY

Abernathy, V.D. (1973) Social network and response to the maternal role. *International Journal of Sociology and Family*, Vol 3, 86-92

Affleck, G. & Tennen, H. (1993). In A. P. Turnbull & H.R. Turnbull (Eds.), *Cognitive coping, families, and disability*, 135-50. Baltimore: Brookes.

Aldwin, C. M. (1994). *Stress, coping, and development: An integrative perspective.* New York: Guilford Press.

American Educational Research Association, American Psychological Association, & National Council on Measurement in Education. (1985). *Standards for educational and psychological testing.* Washington, DC: American Psychological Association, Inc.

Anderson, L., Lakin, C, Managan, T. and Prouty, R. (1998) State institutions: Thirty Years of Depopulation and Closure. *Mental Retardation*, December 1998, v36, no6, p. 431-43

Anderson, R. & Bury, M. (Eds) (1988) Living With Chronic Illness: *The Experience of Patients and their Families.* London: Unwin Hyman

Annual Report From the New York State Commission on Quality of Care for the Mentally Disabled (1997-1998). Albany, New York: Williams and Wilkins, Inc.

Autism Society of America (2004). *Treatment Options.* Retrieved August 8, 2004 from http://www.autism-society.org/site/PageServer?pagename=TreatmentOptions

Barnett, W.S. (1995). *Long-Term Affects of Early Childhood Programs on Cognitive and School Outcomes.* The Future of Children, 5, 3, pp. 1-17

Bauer, S. (1995). Autism and the Pervasive Developmental Disorders: Part 1. *Pediatrics in Review.* 16, 4, pp. 130-136

Bauer, S. (1995). Autism and the Pervasive Developmental Disorders: Part 2. *Pediatrics in Review.* 16, 5, pp. 168-177

Baxter, Christine; Cummins, Robert A.; Yiolitis, Lewi. Jun 2000, Parental stress attributed to family members with and without disability: A longitudinal study. *Journal of Intellectual & Developmental Disability,* Vol. 25 Issue 2, p105, 14p.

Baxter, Christine; Cummins, Robert A.; Yiolitis, Lewi. Jun 2000, *Parental stress attributed to family members with and without disability: A longitudinal study. Journal of Intellectual & Developmental Disability,* Vol. 25 Issue 2, p105, 14p.

Beck, A. T. & Steer, R. A. (1984), Internal consistencies of the original and revised Beck Depression Inventory. *Journal of Clinical Psychology.* 40:1365-1367

Beckman, L. J. (1994). Treatment needs of women with alcohol problems. *Alcohol, Health & Research World,* 18, 206-211

Beckman, P. J. (1991) 'Comparison of Mothers' and Fathers' Perceptions of the Effect of Young Children with and without Disabilities', *American Journal on Mental Retardation* 95: 585–95.

Behr, S.K. & Murphy, D.L. (1993). In A.P. Turnbull & H.R. Turnbull (Eds.), *Cognitive coping, families, and disability,* 1151-164. Baltimore: Brookes.

Bengtson, V., AcCock, A.; Allen, K.; and Klein, D. (2005) *Sourcebook of Family Theory and Research.* London, UK: Sage Publications.

Besharov, D. J. (1992) (September/October). Not all single mothers are created equal. *The American Enterprise,* 13-17

Besharov, D. J. (1992). New directions for Head Start. *Education Digest,* September, Vol. 58 Issue 1, p7, 5p

Birnbaum, A. & Cohen, H.J. (1993) 'On The Importance Of Helping Families: Policy Implications From A National Study', *Mental Retardation* 31: 67–74.

Boss, P. (1988) *Family Stress Management,* Sage Publications

Bouma, R., & Schweitzer, R. (1990). The impact of chronic childhood illness on family stress: A comparison between autism and cystic fibrosis. *Journal of Clinical Psychology,* 46(6), 722-730

Bowen, G.L. (1992). Social Network and the Maternal Role Satisfaction of Formerly Married Mothers. Journal of Divorce, 5, 77 – 83.

Bowen, Murry, (1966) *The Use of Family Theory in Clinical Practice*, as published in *Family Therapy In Clinical Practice*, Copyright © 1985, 1983, 1978 by Jason Aronson, Inc., 1986 Printing

Boyce, G. C., Behl, D., Mortensen, L. & Akers, J. (1991). Child characteristics, family demographics and family processes: Their effects on the stress experienced by families of children with disabilities. *Counseling Psychology Quarterly, 4,* 273–288.

Boyle, M. & Lipman, E. (2005). *Social support and education groups for single mothers: a randomized controlled trial of a community-based program.* Published at www.cmaj.ca on Nov. 17, 2005

Brannan, C., Heflinger, E. and Foster (2003) The role of caregiver strain and other family variables in determining children's use of mental health services. Journal of Emotional and Behavioral Disorders

Bristol, M. (1984) 'Family Resources And Successful Adaptation To Autistic Children', In E. Schopler & G.B. Mesibov (Eds) *The Effects Of Autism On The Family.* New York: Plenum.

Bristol, M. (1987). Mothers of children with autism or communication disorders: Adaptation and the Double ABCX. *Journal of Autism and Developmental Disorders*, 17(4), 469-484.

Bristol, M.M. (1985). Designing programs for young developmentally delayed children: A family systems approach to autism. *Remedial and Special Education*, 4(6), 46-53.

Bristol, M.M., & Schopler, E. (1983). Stress and coping in families of autistic adolescents. In M.E. Schopler & G.B. Mesibov (Eds.), *Autism in adolescents and adults* (pp. 251-278). New York: Plenum Press.

Broman, C. L. (1993). Race differences in marital well-being. *Journal of Marriage and the Family,* 55, 724-732.

Broman, C. L., Riha, M. L., & Trahan, M.R. (1996). Traumatic events and marital well-being. *Journal of Marriage and the Family*, 58, 908-916

Bronstein, P., Clauson, J., Stoll, M. F., & Abrams, C. L. (1993). Parenting behavior and children's social, psychological, and academic adjustment in diverse family structures. *Family Relations, 42,* 268-276.

Brown, I. and Fudge- Schormans, A. (2003) Maltreatment and Life Stressors in Single Mothers Who Have Children with Developmental Delay.

Journal Of Developmental Disabilities, Volume 10, Number 1, pp.61-69

Bryan, T., Pearl, R., & Fallon, P. (1989). Conformity to peer pressure by students with learning disabilities: A replication. Journal of Learning Disabilities, 22, 458-459.

Bryan, T., Werner, M., & Pearl, R. (1982). Learning disabled students' conformity responses to prosocial and antisocial situations. Learning Disability Quarterly, 5, 344-352.

Burden, D. (1986). Single parents and the work setting: The impact of multiple job and home life responsibilities. *Family relations, 35,* 37-43.

Burton, D., & Naylor, S. (1997). Is anxiety really facilitative? Reaction to the myth that cognitive anxiety always impairs sport performance. *Journal of Applied Sport Psychology, 9,* 295-302

Centers for Disease Control Prevention (2004)

Charmaz, K. (1990) "Discovering" Chronic Illness: Using Grounded Theory, *Social Science and Medicine* 11: 1161–72.

Charmaz, K. (1995) 'Grounded Theory', In J.A. Smith, R. Harré, & L. Van Langenhove (Eds) *Rethinking Methods In Psychology.* London: Sage.

Charmaz, K. (2006) Constructing *Grounded Theory: A Practical guide through qualitative analysis.* Thousand Oaks, CA: Sage Publications, Inc.

Cobb, P. S. (1987) 'Creating Respite-Care Programs', *Exceptional Parent* 15(5): 31–3.

Coletta, N.D. (1978) Divorced mothers at two income levels: Stress, support and childrearing practices. *Dissertation Abstracts International,* Vol 38 (12-B, 6114)

Corbin, J., & Strauss, A. (1990). Grounded theory research: Procedures, canons, and evaluative criteria. *Qualitative Sociology, 13*(1), 3-21.

Creswell, J.W. (1998). *Qualitative inquiry and research design: Choosing among the five traditions.* Thousand Oaks, CA: Sage Publications, Inc.

Darling, S. (2004) Needs of and Supports for African American and European American Caregivers of Young Children with Special Needs in Urban and Rural Settings. *Topics in Early Childhood Special Education* v. 24 no2, Summer, p. 98-109

DeMeyer, M. (1979). *Parents and children in Autism.* New York: John Wiley & Sons.

Demo, D. H. (1993). The relentless search for effects of divorce: Forging new trails or tumbling down the beaten path? *Journal of Marriage and the Family, 55,* 42-45.

Denzin, N. K., & Lincoln Y. S. (1994). Entering the field of qualitative research. In N. K. Denzin & Y. S. Lincoln (Eds.), *Handbook of qualitative research* (pp. 1-17). Thousand Oaks, CA: Sage.

Denzin, N. K., & Lincoln, Y. S. (Eds.). (2003). *Strategies of qualitative inquiry* (2nd ed.). Thousand Oaks, CA: Sage.

Dey, I. (1993). *Qualitative data analysis: A user-friendly guide for social scientists.* New York: Routledge.

Dey, I. (1999).*Grounding grounded theory: Guidelines for qualitative inquiry.* San Diego, CA: Academic Press
Diagnostic and Statistical Manual of Mental Disorders – Fourth Edition. (1994) Washington, DC: American Psychiatric Association

Digest of Education Statistics (2002). U.S. Department of Education, Office of Special Education Programs, Data Analysis system (DANS)

Dilworth-Anderson, P., Williams, W. S., & Gibson, B. E. (2002). Issues of race, ethnicity, and culture in care giving research: A 20-year review (1980-2000). *The Gerontologist,* 42, 237-272.

Draper, T.W. & Marcos, A.C. (1990) *Family Variables: Conceptualization, Measurement, and Use.* London: Sage Publications.

Duffy, M. (1995). Factors influencing the health behaviors of divorced women with children. *Journal of Divorce and Remarriage, 22,* 1-12.

Dumas, J.E., Wolf, L.C., Fisman, S.N. & Culligan, A. (1991) 'Parenting Stress, Child Behavior Problems, and Dysphoria in Parents of Children with Autism, Down Syndrome, Behavior Disorders, and Normal Development', *Exceptionality* 2: 97–110.

Dunn, M., Burbine, T., Bowers, C., & Tantleff-Dunn, S. (2001) Moderators of stress in parents of children with Autism. *Community Mental Health Journal, 37*(1), 39-51.

Dunst, C. J., Jenkins, V., & Trivette, C. M. (1984). Family Support Scale: Reliability and validity. *Journal of Individual, Family and Community Wellness*, 1, 45-52.

Dunst, C. J., Trivette, C. M., & Cross, A. H. (1986). Mediating influences of social support: Personal, family, and child outcomes. *American Journal of Mental Deficiency*, 90, 403-417

Dunst, C., Trivette, C., Starnes, A., Hamby, D., & Gordon, N. (1993). *Building and evaluating family support initiatives*. Baltimore: Paul H. Brookes.

Ell, Kathleen. (1996). Crisis theory and social work practice. In Turner, Francis J. (Ed.). *Social work treatment: Interlocking theoretical approaches,* pp. 168-190. New York: The Free Press

Esping-Andersen, G. (1999) "Comparative Welfare Regimes Re-Examined, " *Social Foundations of Postindustrial Economics,* pp. 73-94

Etzel, B. and Leblanc, J. (1979). The Simplest Treatment Alternative: The Law of Parsimony Applied to Choosing Appropriate Instructional Control and Errorless-Learning Procedures for the Difficult-to-teach Child. *Journal of Autism and Developmental Disorders*, 9, 4, pp. 361-383

Featherstone, H. (1982). *A difference in the family: Living with a disabled child.* Ontario: Penguin.

Figley CR, McCubbin M. (1983) *Stress and the family*. New York, Brunner/Mazel
Figley, C. R. (Ed.). (1989). *Treating stress in families* (1st ed.). Levittown, PA: Brunner/Mazel.

Findler, L. (2000) The role of grandparents in the social support system of mothers of children with a physical disability. *Families in Society: The Journal of Contemporary Human Services,* 81 (4) 370-381.

Fisman, S., Wolf, L., & Noh, S. (1989) Marital intimacy in parents of exceptional children. *Canadian Journal of Psychiatry*, 34, 519-525.

Floyd, F. J. & Gallagher, E. M. (1997). Parental stress, care demands, and use of support services for school-age children with disabilities and behavior problems. *Family Relations, 46,* 359–371

Flynn, J. (1982). Report *of the Senate Select Committee on the Handicapped*. Albany, N.Y.: State, MD: Williams and Wilkins, Inc.

Folkman, S. (1992). Making the case for coping. In B. Carpenter (Ed.), *Personal coping: Theory, research, and application* (pp.31-46). Westport, CT: Praeger.

Folkman, S., Lazarus, R. S., Gruen, R., & DeLongis, A. (1986). Appraisal, coping, health status, and psychological symptoms. *Journal of Personality and Social Psychology, 50*, 571-579.

Folkman, S., Schaefer, C., & Lazarus, R. (1979). Cognitive processes as mediators of stress and coping. In V. Hamilton & D. Warburton (Eds.), *Human stress and cognition* (pp. 265-300).New York: John Wiley.

Fudge Schormans, A. (2003). Child maltreatment and developmental disabilities. In I. Brown, & M. Percy (Eds.), *Developmental disabilities in Ontario* (2nd ed.) (pp. 551-582).

Fudge Schormans, A., & Brown, I. (2002). An investigation into the characteristics of the maltreatment of children with developmental delays and the alleged perpetrators of this maltreatment. *Journal on Developmental Disabilities, 8*(1).

Galvan, J. (2007) (3rd ED). *Writing Literature Reviews*. Glendale, C.A.: Pyrczak Publishing

Glaser, B. (2001). Doing grounded theory. *Grounded Theory Review, 2*, 1-18.

Glaser, B. G. (1978). *Theoretical sensitivity: Advances in methodology of grounded theory*. Mill Valley, CA: Sociological Press.

Glaser, B. G. (1992). *Basics of grounded theory analysis*. Mill Valley, CA: Sociological Press.

Glaser, B. G., & Strauss, A. L. (1967). *Discovery of grounded theory: Strategies for qualitative research*. Chicago: Aldine.

Glass, P. (2001) *Autism and the Family: A Qualitative Perspective*. Virginia Tech University Libraries, VA.

Goldberg, G. and Rosenthal, M. (2002) *Diminishing Welfare – A Cross-National Study of Social Provision*. Wesport, Conn.: Auburn House.

Goldberg, W; Greenburger, E.; Hamill, S., & O'Neil, R. (1992). Role demands in the lives of employed single mothers with preschoolers. *Journal of Family Issues, 13*, 312-333.

Gottlieb, S. (2003) US study shows 10-fold increase in autism over the past 20 years. *British Medical Journal*, Vol. 326 Issue 7380, p71

Gray D. & Holden W. (1992) Psychosocial well-being among the parents of children with autism. *Journal of Intellectual Disability*; Vol 45, Issue 6

Gray, D. E. (1993) 'Negotiating Autism: Relations between Parents and Treatment Staff', Social Science and Medicine 36: 1037–46.

Gray, D. E. (1993). Perceptions of stigma: The parents of autistic children. Sociology of Health and Illness, 15(1), 102-120.

Gray, D. E. (1994) 'Coping With Autism: Stresses and Strategies', Sociology of Health and Illness 16: 275–300.

Guion, L.A. (2002) Triangulation: Establishing the Validity of Qualitative Studies. *Florida Cooperative Extension Service, Institute of Food and Agricultural Sciences,* University of Florida. Publication: September 2002.

Hadadian, A. (1994). Stress and social support in fathers and mothers of young children with and without disabilities. *Early Education and Development*, 5, 226-235.

Haefele, W.F., & Henggeler, S.W. (1983). Autism: a family-ecological systems perspective. Paper presented at Meeting Their Needs: Provision of Services to the Severely Emotionally Disturbed and Autistic. Memphis, TN.

Hale, C.J., Hannum, J.W., Espelage, D.L. (2005) Social Support and Physical Health: The Importance of Belonging. *Journal of American College Health.* 53, 6, 276-284.

Hanson, S. M. (1986a). Healthy single-parent families. *Family Relations, 35*, 125-132.

Hanson, S. M. (1986b). Father-child relationships: Beyond Kramer vs. Kramer. *Marriage and Family Review, 9*, 135-149.

Happe, F., & Frith, U. (1991). Is autism a pervasive developmental disorder? Debate and argument: How useful is the PDD label? *Journal of Child Psychology and Psychiatry and Allied Disciplines,* 32, 1167-1168.

Harris, S. (2005) No effect of MMR withdrawal on the incidence of autism: a total population study. *Journal of Child Psychology.* Jun; 46(6):572-9.

Harris, S., Handleman, J., (1994). Preschool education programs for children with autism. Austin: PRO-ED, Inc.

Heatherington, M.E., Cox, M., & Cox, R. (1982). Effects of divorce on parents and children. In M. E. Lamb (Ed.) *Nontraditional Families: Parent and Child Development.* Hillsdale, NJ: Lawrence Erlbaum.

Heller, T., & Factor, A. (1993). Aging family caregivers: Support resources and changes in burden and placement desire. American Journal of Mental Retardation, 98, 417-426.

Heller, T., Miller, A., & Hsieh, K. (1999). Impact of a consumer-directed family support program on adults with developmental disabilities and their family caregivers. *Family Relations*, 48, 419-427.

Hendrickson, G (2000). Stress. http://www.northmemorial.com/HealthEncyclopedia/content/3096.asp . Accessed 11/30/05.

Henwood, K. & Pidgeon, N. (1995) 'Qualitative Research and Psychological Theorizing', *The Psychologist* 3: 115–18.

Hill, R. (1949). *Families under stress: Adjustment to the crises of war separation and reunion.* Westport, CT: Greenwood Press.

Hill, R. (1958). Social stresses on the family: Generic features of families under stress. *Social Casework, 39*, 139-150.

Hilton, J.M., Desrochers, S., & Devall, E.L. (2001).Comparison of role demands, relationships, and child functioning in single-mother, single-father, and intact families.

Hodges, W. F., Buchsbaum, H. K., & Tierney, C. W. (1983). Parent-child relationships and adjustment in preschool children in divorced and intact families. *Journal of Divorce*, 7, 43-59

Hodgson, J.; Dienhart, A. & Daly, K. (2001) Time Juggling: Single Mothers' Experience of Time-Press Following Divorce. *Journal of Divorce & Remarriage,* Vol. 35(1/2)

Holman, T.B. & Burr, W.R. (1980) Beyond the beyond: The growth of family theories in the 1970's. *Journal of Marriage and the Family*, 42, 729-741

Holmes, N. & Carr, J. (1991) 'The Pattern Of Care In Families Of Adults With A Mental Handicap: A Comparison Between Families Of Autistic

Adults And Down Syndrome Adults. *Journal of Autism and Developmental Disorders* 21(2): 159–76.

Holroyd, J., & McArthur, D. (1976). Mental retardation and stress on the parents: A contrast between Down syndrome and childhood autism. *American Journal of Mental Deficiency*, 80, 431-436.

Holroyd, J., Brown, N., Wikler, L., & Simmons, J. (1975) Stress in families of institutionalized and non-institutionalized autistic children. *Journal of Community Psychology*, 3, 26-31.

Horowitz, A. (2004) The *Mediating Effects of perceptions and coping strategies between personal resources and emotional well-being: A study of mothers of children with autism.* Ann Arbor, MI; ProQuest Information and Learning Co.

Howlin, P. & Moore, A. (1997) 'Diagnosis in Autism: A Survey of 1200 Patients in the UK', *Autism* 1: 135–62.

Hulley, S., Cummings, S., and Browner, W. (2001) (2nd ED*) Designing Clinical Research - An Epidemiologic Approach.* Philadelphia, PA: Lippincott Williams & Wilkins, Inc

Hunt, E. and Colander, D (11ed) (2002) *Social Science – An Introduction to the Study of Society.* Boston, MA; Allyn and Bacon Company

Individuals with Disabilities Education Act (2002) US Department of Education Statistics; Washington, DC

Johnston CK, Hessl D, Blasey CM, Eliez S, Erba H, Dyer-Friedman J, Glaser B, Reiss AL (2003). Factors associated with parenting stress in mothers of children with fragile X syndrome." *Journal of Developmental Behavioral Pediatrics.* 24(4):267-275

Journal of Divorce & Remarriage, 35(1/2), 29–56

Joyce, P.A. (2007) The production of therapy: The social Process of Construction of the mother of a Sexually Abused Child. *Journal of Child Sexual Abuse.* Vol.16 (3):1-18

Kamp-Becker, I; Mattejat, F; & Remschmidt, H. (2004). Diagnosis and etiology of Asperger's Syndrome in children and adolescents. *Prax Kinderpsychol und Kinderpsychiatrie.* July-August 2004, 53 (6), 371-94

Kane, R.L., Kane, R. A., Ladd, R. and Veazle, W. (1998) Variation in State Spending for Long-Term care: Factors Associated with More Balanced Systems. *Journal of Health Politics, Policy and Law,* Vol. 23, No. 2, April 1998

Kaplan, M. *(*1994*).* *Role of vision in autism.* Paper presented at the Geneva Centre Symposium, Toronto, Canada

Karger, H.J. and Stoetsz, D. (2002) Chapter 12:" Social Welfare Policy Research: A Framework for Policy Analysis," *American Social Welfare Policy: A Pluralist Approach,* pp. 28-36

Kaufman, A., Campbell, V., & Adams, J. (1990). A lifetime of caring: Older parents who care for adult children with mental retardation. Community Alternatives: *International Journal of Family Care,* 2(1), 39-54.

Key, R. & Sanik, M. (1990). The effects of homemakers' employment status on children's time allocation in single and two-parent families. *Lifestyles, 11,* 71-88

Koegel, R., Schreibman, L., Loos, L., Dirlich-Wilhelm, H., Dunlap, G., Robbins, F., & Plienis, A. Consistent stress profiles in mothers of children with autism. *Journal of Autism and Developmental Disorders,* 1992, 22, 205-216.

Konstantareas, M. M. (1990). A psycho educational model for working with families of autistic children. Journal of Marital and Family Therapy, 16(1), 59-70.

Konstantareas, M., & Homatidis, S. (1989). Assessing child symptom severity and stress in parents of autistic children. *Journal of Child Psychology and Psychiatry and Allied Disciplines,* 30, 459-470.

Konstantareas, M., Homatidis, S., & Plowright, C.M.S. (1992). Assessing resources and stress in parents of severely dysfunctional children. Journal of Autism and Developmental Disorders, 22(2), 217-234.

Koopman, C., Classen, C., Carden, E., & Spiegel, D. (1995). When disaster strikes, acute stress disorder may follow. *Journal of Traumatic Stress, 8,* 1, 29-46.

Krause, N. (2001). Social Support. In R. H. Binstock and L. K. George (Eds.), Handbook of aging and the social sciences (pp. 272-294). San Diego, CA: Academic Press.

Kuhn, T. (3rd Ed.) (1996) *Structure of Scientific Revolutions*. Chicago, Ill: University of Chicago Press

Kummerer, S., Lopez-Reyna, N., & Tejero-Hughes, M. (2007). Mexican Immigrant Mothers' Perceptions of Their Children's Communication Disabilities, Emergent Literacy Development, and Speech-Language Therapy Program. *American Journal of Speech-Language Pathology*; Vol. 16:271–282

La Gaipa, J. J. (1990). The negative effects of informal support systems. In S. Duck (Ed.), *Personal relationships and social support* (pp. 122-139). New York: Sage.

Landsman, Gail H. (1998). "Reconstructing Motherhood in an Age of 'Perfect' Babies: Mothers of Infants and Toddlers with Disabilities," *Signs* 24(1): 69-99

Lazarus, R. S. & Cohen, J. B. (1977). Environmental stress. In I. Altman & J. F. Wohlwill (Eds.), *Human behavior and the environment:* Current theory and research (pp. 89-127). New York: Plenum Press.

Lazarus, R. S. (1980). The stress and coping paradigm. In C. Eidorfer, D. Cohen, & AKleinman (Eds.), *Conceptual models for psychopathology* (pp. 173-209). New York: Spectrum

Lazarus, R.S. & Folkman, S. (1984) *Stress, appraisal, and coping*. New York: Springer Verlag.

Lazarus, R.S. (1966). *Psychological stress and the coping process*. New York: McGraw-Hill.

Lero, D. & Brockman, L. (1993). Single parent families in Canada: A closer look. In J. Hudson & B. Galaway (Eds.) *Single parent families: Perspectives on research and policy*. Toronto: Thompson Educational Publishing.

Lieberman MA, Borman LD (1979): Self-Help Groups for Coping with Crisis. Jossey-Bass Inc., San Francisco

Lilly-J.D; Reed-D; Wheeler-K.G (2003). Perceptions of psychological contract violations in school districts that serve children with autism spectrum disorder: an exploratory qualitative study. *Journal-of-Applied-School-Psychology.* 20(1): 27-45

Lincoln, Y.S., & Guba, E.G. (1985). *Naturalistic inquiry*. Beverly Hills, CA: Sage Publications.

Lindblom, C. E. and Woodhouse, E.J. (1993) Chapter 11: "Making the Most of Analysis," *ThePolicy Making Process*, pp. 126-150.

London, R.A. (1996). The difference between divorced and never married mothers' participation in the Aid to Families with Dependent children program. *Journal of Family Issues, 17*(2), 7-22

Lovaas, O.I. (1979). Contrasting Illness and Behavioral Models for the Treatment of Autistic Children: A Historical Perspective. *Journal of Autism and Developmental Disorders.* 9, 4, pp. 315-323.

Lustig, D. & Thomas, K. (1997). Adaptation of families to the entry of young adults with mental retardation into supported employment. *Education and Training in Mental Retardation and Developmental Disabilities, 32,* 21–31.

Marcus, L., Schopler, E., and Lord, C. (2000). TEACCH services for preschool children. *In Preschool Education Programs for Children with Autism, J.S. Handelman and S.L. Harris* (eds.)., Austin, TX: Pro-Ed.

Marcus, L.M., Kunce, L.J. & Schopler, E. (1997) 'Working with Families', In D. J. Cohen & F.R. Volkmar (Eds) *Handbook of Autism and Pervasive Developmental Disorders*. New York: Wiley.

Matt, JA , Wethington E , Kessler RC . (1990) Situational determinants of coping and coping effectiveness. *Journal of Health & Social. Behavior.* 31:103–22

Mayer, R. R. (1985) Policy and Program Planning: A Developmental Perspective. Englewood Cliffs, New Jersey: Prentice Hall

McCubbin HI, Patterson JM. Systemic assessment of family stress, resources and coping: Tools for research, education and clinical intervention. St. Paul, Minnesota, Department of Family Social Science; 1981.

McCubbin M, McCubbin H. (1993) Families coping with illness: The resiliency model of family stress, adjustment, and adaptation. Madison, Wisconsin, University of Wisconsin-Madison;

McCubbin, H., Thompson, A., & McCubbin, M. (1996). *Family assessment: Resiliency, coping and adaptation--inventories for research and practice*. Madison, WI: University of Wisconsin System.

McCubbin, M. & Patterson, J. (1983) The family stress process: The double ABCX model of adjustment and adaptation. *Social Stress and the*

Family: Advances and developments in family stress theory and research. New York: Haworth.

McCubbin, M., & McCubbin, H. (1991). Family stress theory and assessment: The Resiliency Model of Family Stress, Adjustment and Adaptation. In H. I. McCubbin & A. I. Thompson (Eds.), *Family Assessment inventories for research and practice* (pp. 3-32). Madison, WI: University of Wisconsin.

McCubbin, Marilyn A., & McCubbin, Hamilton, I. (1989). Theoretical Orientations to Family Stress and Coping. In C.R. Figley, Ph.D. (Ed.), Treating *stress in families (*pp. 3-43). Levittown, PA: Brunner/Mazel, Inc.

McCullough, J. & Zick, C. D. (1992). The roles of role strain, economic resources, and time demands in explaining mothers' life satisfaction. *Journal of Family and Economic issues,* 13, 23-44.

McKaig, K. (1986). *Beyond the Threshold: Families Caring for their Children Who Have Significant Developmental Disabilities.* New York, NY: Community Service Society of New York.

McLanahan, S. & Booth, K. (1989). Mother-only families: Problems, prospects, and politics. *Journal of Marriage and the Family, 51,* 557-580.

Michie, S., Mcdonald, V. & Marteau, T. (1996) 'Understanding Responses to Predictive Genetic Testing: A Grounded Theory Approach', *Psychology and Health* 11: 455–70.

Midence, K. & O'Neill, M. (1999) The experiences of parents in the diagnosis of Autism: A Pilot Study. *Autism,* Vol. 3, P. 273-285

Milardo, R. M. (1987). Changes in social networks of women and men following divorce. *Journal of Family Issues, 8,* 79-96

Milgram, N., & Atzil, M. (1988). Parenting Stress in Raising Autistic Children. *Journal of Autism and Developmental Disorders,* 18(3), 415-424

Miller, A. C; Gordon, R. M.; Daniele, R. J. and Diller, L. (1992). Stress, Appraisal, and Coping in Mothers of Disabled and Nondisabled Children. *Journal of Pediatric Psychology* 17(5) pp. 587-605

Miller, D (1993). *Teaching adolescent females with behavioral/emotional disorders, adolescent offenders, and adolescents at risk: A literature-based approach.* Reston. Va.: ERIC Document Reproduction Service.

Miller, D. (1993). The literature project: Using literature to improve the self-concept of at-risk adolescent females. *Journal of Reading* 36: 442-48.

Monette, D.; Sullivan, T.; & DeJong, C. (2002) (5th Ed.) *Applied Social Research – Tool for the Human Services.* Wadsworth/Thompson Learning Publishers.

Morgan, S. B. (1988). The autistic child & family functioning: A developmental family systems perspective. Journal of Autism and Developmental Disorders, 18(2), 263-280.

Moroz, K.J. (1989). Educating Autistic Children and Youths: A School-Family-Community Partnership. (Winter 1989) *Social Work in Education*, 4, pp.107-124

Moxely, D.P. and Jacobs, D.R. (1995) The Role of Animation as a Program Development Strategy. *Administration in Social Work,* 19 (1), pp. 1-13

Newsome, W. (2000) Parental perceptions during periods of transition: Implications for social workers serving families coping with autism. *Journal of Family Social Work*, 5(2), 17-31.

Norton, P. & Drew, C. (1994) 'Autism and Potential Family Stressors'. *The American Journal of Family Therapy* 22: 67–76.
Olsen, M.B. & Hwang, C.P. (2002) Sense of Coherence in Parents. *Journal of Intellectual Disability Research.* Volume 46 Part 7, 548-559.

Orr, R. R., Cameron, S. J. & Day, D. M. (1991). Coping with stress in families with children who have mental retardation: An evaluation of the Double ABCX model. *American Journal of Mental Retardation, 95,* 444–450.

Padgett, D. K. (1998) *Qualitative Methods in Social Work Research – Challenges and Rewards.* Thousand Oaks, California: SAGE Publications

Patterson, J. (2002). Integrating Family Resilience and Family Stress Theory *Journal of Marriage & the Family*, Vol. 64, Issue 2

Pearl, R., & Bryan, T. (1992). Students' expectations about peer pressure to engage in misconduct. *Journal of Learning Disabilities*, 25, 582-585, 597.

Pearl, R., Bryan, T., & Herzog, A. (1990). Resisting or acquiescing to peer pressure to engage in misconduct: Adolescents' expectations of probable consequences. *Journal of Youth and Adolescence*, 19, 43-55.

Pearl, R., Bryan, T., Fallon, P., & Herzog, A. (1991). Learning disabled students' detection of deception. *Learning Disabilities Research and Practice*, 6, 12-16.

Pearl, R., Donahue, M., & Bryan, T. (1985). The development of tact: Children's strategies for delivering bad news. Journal of Applied Developmental Psychology, 6, 141-149.

Pearlin, L. I., & Skaff, M. M. (1998). Perspectives on the family and stress in late life. In J. Lomranz (Ed.), Handbook of aging and mental health (pp. 323-340). New York: Plenum

Pearlin, L. I., Mullan, J. T., Semple, S. J., & Skaff, M. M. (1990). Caregiving and the stress process: An overview of concepts and their measure. The Gerontologist, 30, 583-594.

Pearlin, L.I., & Schooler, C. (1978). The structure of coping. *Journal of Health and Social Behavior*, 22, 337-356

Pervin, L.A. and John, O.P. (2001) Personality: Theory and Research (8th ED). New York: John Wiley & Sons, Inc.

Pillemer, K., Moen, P., Wellington, E., & Glasgow, N. (2000). Introduction. In K. Pillemer, P. Moen, E. Welhington, & N. Glasgow (Eds.), Social integration in the second half of life (pp. 19-47). Baltimore, MD: Johns Hopkins University Press.

Piper, E. & Howlin, P. (1992) 'Assessing And Diagnosing Developmental Disorders That Are Not Evident At Birth: Parental Evaluations Of Intake Procedures', *Child: Care, Health And Development* 18: 35–55.

Piven, J., Chase, G., Landa, R., & Wzorek, M. (1991) Psychiatric disorders in the parents of autistic individuals. *Journal of the American Academy of Child and Adolescent Psychiatry*, 30, 471-478.

Polkinghorne, D. (1983) *Methodology for the Human Sciences – Systems of Inquiry.* Pages 244-258.

Powers, M. Psy.D. (1989). *Children with Autism – A Parents' Guide.* Rockville, MD: Woodbine House.

Quine, L. & Rutter, D.R. (1994) 'First Diagnosis of Severe Mental and Physical Disability: A Study of Doctor–Parent Communication', *Journal of Child Psychology and Psychiatry* 35: 1273–87.

Quinn, P., & Allen, K. R. (1989). Facing challenges and making compromises: How single. mothers endure. Family Relations, 38, 390-395

Raif, R., & Rimmerman, A. (1993). Parental attitudes to out-of-home placement of young children with developmental disabilities. *International Journal of Rehabilitation Research*, 16, 97-105.

Reis, H. & Franks, P. (1994) The role of intimacy and social support in health outcomes: Two processes or one? Personal Relationships. Volume 1 Page 185: June

Richards, L. N. (1989). The precarious survival and hard-won satisfactions of white single parent families. *Family Relations, 38*, 396-403.

Roberts, M., Lazicki-Puddy, T, Puddy, R; and Johnson, R. (2003) The outcomes of psychotherapy with adolescents: A Practitioner-Friendly Research Review. *Journal of Clinical Psychology*, 59, November, 1177-1191.

Rodrigue, J. R. (1992). Psychosocial adaptation of fathers of children with autism, Down syndrome, and normal development. *Journal of Autism and Developmental Disorders*, 22(2), 249-263.

Rodrigue, J.R., Morgan, S.B., & Geoffken, G. Families of autistic children: Psychological functioning of mothers. *Journal of Clinical Psychology*, 1990, Vol. 19, 371-379.

Rousey, A. M., Best, S. & Blacher, J. (1992). Mothers and fathers perceptions of stress and coping with children who have severe disabilities. *American Journal of Mental Retardation, 97,* 99–109.

Said, E. (1978) *Orientalism.* New York; Pantheon Books.

Said, E. and Vishwanthan, G. (2001) *Power, Politics and Culture – Interviews with Edward W. Said.* New York; Pantheon Books.

Salisbury, C. L. (1990). Characteristics of users and nonusers of respite care. *Mental Retardation*, 28, 291-297.

Sanders, J. L., & Morgan, S. B. (1997). Family stress and management as perceived by parents of children with autism or Down syndrome:

Implications for intervention. *Child and Family Behavior Therapy*, 19, 15-32.

Sanik, M. & Maudlin, T. (1986). Single versus two-parent families: A comparison of mother's time. *Family Relations, 35*, 53-65.

Schiling, R., Kirkham, M., Snow, W. and Schinke, S. (1986) Single mothers with handicapped children: Different from their counterparts? *Family Relations*, Vol 35, 69-77

Schopler, E., Reichler, R. J., DeVellis, R. F., & Daly, K. (1980). Toward the objective classification of childhood autism: Childhood Autism Rating Scale (CARS). *Journal of Autism and Developmental Disorders*, 10, 91-103.

Scorgie, K, Wilgosh, L, Sobsey, D. and McDonald, J (2001) Parent Life Management and Transformational Outcomes When a Child Has Down syndrome. *International Journal of Special Education.* Vol 16, No.2

Scorgie, K., Wilgosh, L., & McDonald, L. (1996). A qualitative study of managing life when a child has a disability. *Developmental Disabilities Bulletin, 24(2),* 68-90.

Scorgie, K., Wilgosh, L., & McDonald, L. (1997). A survey follow-up on managing life when a child has a disability. *Developmental Disabilities Bulletin, 25(2),* 65-69.

Selye, H. (1956) *The Stress of Life*. New York: McGraw-Hill

Sen, A. (1999) Development as Freedom. New York, N.Y.: Anchor Books

Shapiro, J., Blacher, J. & Lopez, S. R. (1998). Maternal reactions to children with mental retardation. In: Burak, J. A., Hodapp, R. M. & Zigler, R., eds. *Handbook of Mental Retardation and Development*, pp. 606–636. Cambridge University Press, New York.

Sharpley, C., Bitsika, V., & Efremidis, B. (1997). Influence of gender, parental health, and expertise upon stress among parents of children with autism. *Journal of Intellectual and Developmental Disabilities*, 22, 19-28.

Sharpley, C.F., Bitsika, V., & Efremidis, B. (1997) Influence of gender, parental health and perceived expertise of assistance upon stress, anxiety and depression among parents of children with autism. *Journal of Intellectual & Developmental Disability,* Vol. 22, 19-28.

Shea, TM, & Bauer, AM (1991). *Parents and teachers of children with exceptionalities* (2nd Ed.). Boston: Allyn & Bacon

Sherwood, D. (1996). *Crisis Theory and Intervention.* http://www3.baylor.edu/CFCM/ResourcesPDFs/CrisisTheory&Intervention.pdf Accessed 11/28/05.

Shin, J. & Crittenden, K. (2003) Well-being of mothers of children with mental retardation: An evaluation of the Double ABCX model in a cross-cultural context. *Asian Journal of Social Psychology.* Vol.6:171–184

Siegel, B. (1997) 'Coping with the Diagnosis of Autism', In D. J. Cohen & F.R. Volkmar (Eds) *Handbook of Autism and Pervasive Developmental Disorders.* New York: Wiley.

Simpson, R.L. (1995). Individualized Education Programs for Students with Autism: Including he Parents in the Process. *Focus on Autistic Behavior*, October 1995, 10, 4, p. 11-16

Skinner, D., Bailey, D. B., Correa, V., & Rodriguez, P. (1999). Narrating self and disability: Latino mothers' constructions of identities vis-à-vis their child with special needs. *Exceptional Children, 5*, 481-495

Slipp, S. (1988). *The Techniques and Practice of Object Relations Family Therapy.* Chap 1, 2, & 5, pp. 3-44, 83-100

Sloper, P. & Turner, S. (1993) 'Determinants of Parental Satisfaction with Disclosure of Disability', *Developmental Medicine and Child Neurology* 35: 816–25.

Small, S. A., Eastman, G., & Cornelius, S. (1988). Adolescent autonomy and parental stress. *Journal of Youth and Adolescence*, 17, 377-399

Spano, N.A. (1987). *Return to Go: A Look at State spending for community residences for mentally disablDe persons.* Albany, NY: New York State Senate Committee on Mental Hygiene

Stone, W. L., Lee, E. B., Ashford, L., & Brissie, J., Hepburn, S. L., Coonrod, E., & Weiss, B. H. (1999). Can autism be diagnosed accurately in children under 3 years? *Journal of Child Psychology and Psychiatry, 40, 219-226.*

Stone, W. L., Ousley, O. Y., Hepburn, S. L., Hogan, K. L., & Brown, C. S. (1999). Patterns of adaptive behavior in very young children with autism. *American Journal on Mental Retardation*, 104, 187-199.

Strauss, A. (1987). *Qualitative analysis for Social Scientists*. Cambridge, UK: Cambridge University Press.

Strauss, A. (1993) (2nd ED) *Qualitative Analysis for Social Scientists*. New York: Cambridge University Press.

Strauss, A., & Corbin, J. (1990). *Basics of qualitative research: Grounded theory procedures and techniques*. Newbury Park, CA: Sage

Strauss, A., & Corbin, J. (1994). Grounded theory methodology. In N. K. Denzin & Y. S. Lincoln (Eds.), *Handbook of qualitative research* (pp. 273-285). Thousand Oaks, CA: Sage.

Strauss, A., & Corbin, J. (1998). *Basics of qualitative research: Techniques and procedures for developing grounded theory* (2nd Ed.). Thousand Oaks, CA: Sage.

Sugarman, S.D. (2003). Single parent families. In M.A. Mason, A. Skolnick, & S.D. Sugarman (Eds.), *All our families: New policies for a new century* (2nd ed., pp.14–39). New York: Oxford University Press

Sullivan, R.C. (1997) 'Diagnosis Autism: You Can Handle It!' In D. J. Cohen & F.R. Volkmar (Eds) *Handbook of Autism and Pervasive Developmental Disorder*. New York: Wiley.

Tein, J. Y., Sandler, I. N., & Zautra, A. J. (2000). Stressful Life Events, Psychological Distress, Coping, and Parenting of Divorced Mothers: A Longitudinal Sturdy. Journal of Family Psychology, 14, 27 - 41.

Thoits (1986) Social Support, Appraisals of Events Controllability, Coping. *Journal of Personality and Social Psychology*, 66, 06, 1094-1102.

Thoits, P. A. (1995). Stress, coping and social support processes: Where are we? What next? *Journal of Health and Social Behavior*, 53-79.

Thornton, Serene & Garrett, Kendra J. (1995) Ethnography as a Bridge to Multicultural Practice. *Journal of Social Work Education*, Winter95, Vol. 31 Issue 1, 67-75

Tobing, L (2004) Stress, Coping, and Psychological Distress of Mothers of children with Pervasive Developmental Disorders. *Dissertation Proquest Inc*.: Ann Arbor, MI

Todd, S., & Shearn, J. (1996) Time and the person: The impact of support services on the lives of parents of adults with intellectual disabilities.

Journal of Applied Research in Intellectual Disabilities, Vol. 9, 40-60.

Turnbull, H. R., Bateman, D. F., & Turnbull, A. P. (1993). Families and empowerment. In P. Wehman (Ed.), *The ADA mandate for social change* (pp. 154-174). Baltimore: Brookes.

Turner, F. (1996) *Interlocking Theoretical Approaches - Social Work Treatment.* New York, NY; The Free Press.

Turpin, G., Barley, V., Beail, N., Scaife, J., Slade, P., Smith, J.A. & Walsh, S. (1997) 'Standards For Research Projects And Theses Involving Qualitative Methods: Suggested Guidelines For Trainees And Courses'. *Clinical Psychology Forum* 108: 3–7. 285

U.S Census Bureau – *U.S Department of Education Office of Special Education Programs Data Analysis Systems* (2000) Washington. DC.

United States Census Bureau. (2005). *American Families and Living Arrangements*, June 2005. Washington, D.C: Fields, J & Casper

Van Berckelaer-Onnes, I (2004) Sixty Years of Autism. *Nederlands Tijdschrift voor geneeskunde.* 148 (21), May, 1024-30.

Vaughn, B., Egeland, B. and Sroufe, L.A. (1979). Individual differences in infant mother attachment at twelve and eighteen months: Stability and change in families under stress. *Child Development*, Vol 50, 971-975.

Walker, D. & Myrick, F. (2006) Grounded Theory: An Exploration of Process and Procedure. *Qualitative Health Research*, Vol. 16 No. 4, April, 547-559

Webster-Stratton C, Kolpacoff M, Hollinsworth T (1989). Self-administered videotaped therapy for families with conduct problem children: comparison of two cost-effective treatments and a control group. *Journal of Consulting Clinical Psychology*; 57:550-3.

Weintraub, M. and Wolf, B. (1983) Effects of stress and social supports on mother-child interactions in single and two parent families. *Child Development*, Vol 54, 1297-1311

Weiss, L. (1998) Chapter 1: The State is Dead: Long Live the State, *The Myth of the Powerless State.* Pp. 1-13, 213-214.

Weissman, H.H. (1978) Toward a Social Psychology of Program Design, *Administration in Social Work*, 2(1), pp. 3-14

White, N. and Hastings, R. (2004) Social and Professional Support for Parents of Adolescents with Severe Intellectual Disabilities. *Journal of Applied Research in Intellectual Disabilities* 17:3, 181-190

Williams, S. W., & Dilworth-Anderson, P. (2002). Systems of social support in families who care for dependent African American elders. The Genmtologist, 42, 224-236.

Zeanah, C. (2000) (2nd ED) *Handbook on Infant Mental Health.* New York, NY; The Guilford Press.

Zelkowitz, P. (April 1987) Social Support and Aggressive Behavior in Young Children. *Family Relations*, Vol 36, 129-134.

Made in the USA
Charleston, SC
03 May 2010